Photo Credits

CHAPTER 1

Page 1: Top left: © Ximagination/Dreamstime.com; Top right: © Sebcz/Dreamstime.com; Bottom left: © Janos Gehring/Shutterstock; Bottom right: © Jon Riley/Getty Images

CHAPTER 2

Page 19: Left: © Timnichols1956/Dreamstime.com; Center: © Yellow Dog Productions/Getty Images; Right: © Monkey Business Images/Shutterstock

CHAPTER 3

Page 31: Top left: © PhotostoGO; Top right: © Kablonk! Kablonk!/Photolibrary; Bottom left: © Eric O'Connell/Photolibrary; Bottom right: © PhotostoGO

CHAPTER 4

Page 49: Top left: © Factoria singular fotographia/Shutterstock; Top right: © Futuredigitaldesign (Christopher Futcher)/Dreamstime.com; Bottom left: © Icyimage/Dreamstime.com; Bottom right: © STOCK4B-RF/Getty Images

CHAPTER 5

Page 67: © Matthias Stolt/Photolibrary
Page 69: © Joeshmo/Dreamstime.com

CHAPTER 6

Page 89: Top left: © John A. Rizzo/Getty Images; Top right: © Commercial Eye/Getty Images; Bottom left: © Lonnie Duka/Photolibrary; Bottom right: © Jupiterimages/Getty Images

CHAPTER 7

Page 105: Top left: © Yuri_arcurs/Dreamstime.com; Top right: © Monkey Business Images/Shutterstock; Bottom left: © Mwproductions/Dreamstime.com; Bottom right: © Monkeybusinessimages/Dreamstime.com

CHAPTER 8

Page 123: Left: © PhotostoGO; Right: © Stephane Gautier/Photolibrary

CHAPTER 9

Page 147: Top left: © Prairierattler/Dreamstime.com; Top right: © Raytags/Dreamstime.com; Bottom left: © Yanirta/Dreamstime.com; Bottom right: © Nicolas Sutcliffe/Shutterstock

CHAPTER 10

Page 157: Top left: © John Eder/Getty Images; Top right: © Ustyujanin/Dreamstime.com; Center left: © Snegireva/Dreamstime.com; Center right: © Macduff Everton/Getty Images; Bottom left: © Futuredigitaldesign (Christopher Futcher)/Dreamstime.com; Bottom right: © Barry Willis/Getty Images

Contents

THEMES & TOPICS	PAGE	FUNCTIONS & TASKS	SPEAKING STRATEGIES
		Asking for Information	
CHAPTER 1 How Often Do You Do That?	1	• Buying and selling items	• Speaking versus writing: Special strategies for conversations • Asking for repetition • Speaking politely: Conversations with a beginning, a middle, and an end
CHAPTER 2 Where Can I Find That?	19	• Asking for personal information • Giving directions	• Getting someone's attention • Review: Asking for repetition
		Talking about Habits	
CHAPTER 3 I'm a Very Healthy Person.	31	• Talking about diet, exercise, and other habits	• Real speaking versus writing • Speak, respond, react • Sentence parts
CHAPTER 4 Can I Make a Suggestion?	49	• Talking about study habits • Giving suggestions	• Hedging • Speaking politely: Conversations have a beginning, a middle, and an end
		Asking for Help and Permission	
CHAPTER 5 Is That Really Necessary?	67	• Expressing necessity/obligation and asking for help • Making appointments	• Speaking politely: Conversations with a beginning, a middle, and an end • Hesitation strategies
CHAPTER 6 Could I Borrow This?	87	• Explaining problems • Requesting permission	• Ways of saying *thank you* and *you're welcome* • Starting and ending polite requests • Making a polite request on the telephone • Clarity and politeness in voice messages

On Speaking Terms 2

REAL LANGUAGE FOR REAL LIFE

ELIANA SANTANA-WILLIAMSON
YVONNE CRANMER

HEINLE
CENGAGE Learning™

Australia • Brazil • Japan • Korea • Mexico • Singapore • Spain • United Kingdom • United States

On Speaking Terms 2:
Real Language for Real Life
Eliana Santana-Williamson
Yvonne Cranmer

Publisher: Sherrise Roehr
Acquisitions Editor: Tom Jefferies
Development Editor: Marissa Petrarca
Director, US Marketing: Jim McDonough
Marketing Manager: Caitlin Driscoll
Content Project Manager: Andrea Bobotas
Print Buyer: Susan Spencer
Composition: Pre-Press PMG
Cover Designer: Muse Group, Inc.
Cover Image: Corbis

Library of Congress Control Number: 2009935644

ISBN-13: 978-0-618-39602-3

ISBN-10: 0-618-39602-0

Heinle
20 Channel Center Street
Boston, MA 02210
USA

Cengage Learning is a leading provider of customized learning solutions with office locations around the globe, including Singapore, the United Kingdom, Australia, Mexico, Brazil, and Japan. Locate your local office at: **international.cengage.com/region**

Cengage Learning products are represented in Canada by Nelson Education, Ltd.

Visit Heinle online at **elt.heinle.com**
Visit our corporate website at **cengage.com**

Printed in the United States of America
1 2 3 4 5 6 7 8 9 10 — 13 12 11 10 09

LISTENING STRATEGIES	PRONUNCIATION	GRAMMAR	CONTEXT
		Asking for Information	
• Listening to how people ask for repetition	• Rising and falling intonation	• Simple present tense and adverbs of frequency • Using collocations • Collocations with *get* and *go*	SOCIAL
• Asking for and following directions	• Intonation for *Yes/No* questions with modals	• Using modals to ask for personal information	SOCIAL
		Talking about Habits	
• Listening for sentence stress	• Sentence Stress • Stressing words in sentences	• Review: Simple present tense • Simple present tense and the third-person singular • Simple present tense: Asking and answering negative questions	SOCIAL
• Review: Listening for sentence stress and intonation	• Review: Sentence stress and intonation	• Giving suggestions with and without modals	ACADEMIC
		Asking for Help and Permission	
• Listening for the main idea	• Reductions (reduced forms)	• Explaining necessity and obligation • Asking for help • Responding to requests for help • Making appointments	SOCIAL
• Answering questions when listening for main ideas	• Review: Reductions (reduced forms)	• Making polite requests (asking for permission) • Making promises	ACADEMIC

Contents

THEMES & TOPICS	PAGE	FUNCTIONS & TASKS	SPEAKING STRATEGIES
		Talking about the Past	
CHAPTER 7 I Used to do that.	105	• Describing past events • Giving excuses	• Using encouragers • Self-monitoring your speech
CHAPTER 8 Tell Me a Little about Yourself.	123	• Describing past events and experiences	• Asking for clarification
		Making Plans	
CHAPTER 9 What Are You Going to Do Next Weekend?	141	• Future possibilities and plans	• Connecting thoughts with: *and, and then, 'cause, but,* and *though*
CHAPTER 10 Would You Like to Come?	157	• Inviting • Making plans	• Talking around a word

LISTENING STRATEGIES	PRONUNCIATION	GRAMMAR	CONTEXT
		Talking about the Past	
• Using adverbs to identify tense	• Pronouncing *-ed* • Pronouncing *used to*	• Talking about past events • Contrasting past and present with *used to*	SOCIAL
• Listening to contextual clues	• Word stress	• Review: *Yes/No* questions with simple past • *Wh-* questions with the simple past • Talking about past experiences using the present perfect • Questions in the present perfect tense • Negative statements in the present perfect tense	ACADEMIC
		Making Plans	
• Review: Understanding main ideas	• Reductions (reduced forms) with *will* • Reductions (reduced forms) with *going to*	• Talking about future possibilities • Talking about future plans	SOCIAL
• Review: Using context clues	• Stress and reductions (reduced forms)	• Describing activities with *go* and *-ing* action verbs • Using invitation phrases • Review: Making excuses using the present, past, and future tenses • Review: Using modals to express necessity, obligation, and promises • Expressing certainty and uncertainty	ACADEMIC

To the Instructor

On Speaking Terms: Real Language for Real Life is a book that introduces the English Language Learner to *spoken language the way it is actually spoken*, that is, with its hesitations, pauses, grammar, and sounds present. Traditionally, listening and speaking textbooks have dialogs, or "spoken texts," that are scripted based on how the writers believe spoken language is constructed. ***On Speaking Terms,*** however, exposes learners to features of **real language,** such as, how to hesitate, how to ask for repetition, how to use grammar for speaking, how to connect thoughts as you speak, and many others.

FEATURES OF *ON SPEAKING TERMS*

REAL LIFE

On Speaking Terms is based on **real life** language. Researchers have recorded, transcribed, and analyzed real life interactions and have found that those real life interactions look very different from the spoken texts (dialogs) that appear in traditional speaking textbooks. Real life language does not "look" as "neat and perfect" as shown in most textbooks. For example, speakers don't always speak in complete sentences. When talking, we don't always say a sentence and then wait for the other speaker to say another sentence. That kind of "ping-pong" talk is not realistic. In real life, one speaker tends to dominate the conversation, whereas the listener acknowledges that he or she is listening with sounds and expressions, such as, *uh-huh, yeah, ok, right*, and so forth. In addition, speakers interrupt each other and talk at the same time. Speakers also react to what others say with expressions such as "you're kidding!" or "no way!" These are only a few of the features of real life language addressed in ***On Speaking Terms.***

Chapters 1, 2, 3, 5, 7 and 9 present learners with language they can use within a social context, that is, in and around the community in which they live. They learn how to, for example, talk to friends and people they know, as well as speak politely and more formally with people they don't know. In Chapters 4, 6, 8 and 10, learners are also exposed to language within an academic context, that is, language that can be used in and around the school and workplace to communicate with their instructors, counselors, classmates, and managers.

REAL SPEAKING

Throughout ***On Speaking Terms*** learners are exposed to **real speaking** as they learn the grammar and features of speech. At the same time, they learn *how to be polite* as they use that grammar to communicate. In fact, some research studies show that pragmatics or appropriateness (politeness) mistakes are taken much more seriously by expert speakers of the language than grammatical mistakes are. Corpus linguistics studies also show that politeness is embedded in conversation. In fact, a researcher has stated that "conversation is expressive of politeness." Every chapter of ***On Speaking Terms*** contains Cultural Notes to help the English language learner understand how certain concepts are realized in American culture, and, how those concepts can be incorporated into speech.

REAL GRAMMAR

Another unique feature of ***On Speaking Terms*** is its **real grammar** presentation. Traditionally, textbooks that claim to teach speaking do not overtly teach grammar. Learners are put in groups, asked to discuss issues, and must attempt to construct spoken texts. In ***On Speaking Terms,*** however, learners study *the grammar of speaking*. Although many of the structures utilized in writing and in speaking are the same, grammar of spoken texts can be quite different from that of written texts.

In ***On Speaking Terms,*** you will notice that the structure of the language is presented in boxes. These boxes help learners visualize the arrangement of the linguistic components. Each part of speech (subject, verb, complement, etc.) is presented in a unique box. These boxes represent manipulatives (pieces that users can move around, or, manipulate). By having a mental picture of how grammar works, learners can manipulate the grammar for speaking and apply it to a vast number of situations, allowing them to be able to process grammar more quickly.

REAL LISTENING

Not only does ***On Speaking Terms*** introduce learners to real speech, but it also introduces students to **real listening.** Traditionally, listening is a skill that is tested only rather than taught. In most texts, learners listen to a conversation and answer comprehension questions. An outstanding feature of this textbook is *the teaching of listening*. Learners are introduced to concepts that promote real listening, such as making mental pictures as they listen to the main idea. If learners can figure out how to best process and remember main ideas, they will have a better chance to succeed when they are asked to answer question about these main ideas. Rather than just listening for key facts, learners are taught how to mentally process and remember what they listen to.

Many of the listening tasks in ***On Speaking Terms*** ask student to listen **before** they complete an exercise. These types of listening tasks provide learners with a sample of how people talk when doing a similar task. By listening to that model before they actually do the task, learners can participate in conversations with more confidence.

ORGANIZATION OF *ON SPEAKING TERMS*

CHAPTERS

On Speaking Terms has ten chapters. In Chapters 1, 2, 3, 5, 7, and 9, learners will be exposed to and learn how to engage in short social interactions and service encounters in the community where they live. Chapters 4, 6, 8, and 10 focus on the same skills from the preceding chapter, but students will use that language in the community where they study and work.

Each Chapter contains four distinct sections:

GET STARTED

Get Started introduces the learner to the context of the chapter by having learners look at a picture, listen to a conversation, and complete a simple task. Learners should then be able to start making connections between the new content of the chapter and what is already familiar to them. When learners can connect a new concept to what they already know, they can begin to identify information that is new to them.

LEARN AND PRACTICE

Learn and Practice is divided into four sections: Grammar, Speaking Strategies, Listening Strategies, and Pronunciation. It presents each new concept through scaffolding, and gives learners the opportunity to understand, process and practice the new concept in steps. Learners are presented with language (input) and are required to produce language as well (output). As they produce the language, the instructor has a chance to listen to the learners' language and give them feedback.

Grammar sections visually present the structure of the language. The elements that compose the structure of the language are presented in boxes which are moved around to show how the language works. The boxes are kept consistent throughout the book so learners can remember them. This should help any learner from any linguistic and cultural background remember how the English grammar of speaking works. Learners are asked to use grammar in different contexts (for example, at home or at school) and with different speakers (for example, with a friend or with an instructor) as well.

Speaking Strategies show learners strategies they can use to construct the language as they communicate. When we talk, we need to be able to listen to the speaker, understand the language, construct what we want to say, and say it. Oral communication can be quite complex, but there are strategies that can be used to lessen the burden and which will aid us in doing all these things in a matter of seconds. These strategies are taught throughout the book.

Listening Strategies introduce learners to strategies that can be used to help students listen and successfully process what they are hearing.

Pronunciation activities invite learners to notice how the mouth moves, rather than memorize phonetic symbols. By noticing how the mouth moves, learners should be able to process the information in a more efficient way. In addition, by learning to observe how the language is produced, learners become more independent and may be able to apply those strategies when out of the classroom.

REVIEW AND EXPAND

Learners will engage in simulations, role-plays, and games that provide them with a chance to expand the concepts learned to other contexts.

EVALUATION

Self-Evaluation aims to help learners develop their metacognitive skills. Therefore, learners will reflect upon their learning by checking how well they performed the particular skills taught in that chapter. It will invite the learner to think about what they need to work on and help them design an action plan for improvement.

SUPPLEMENTS FOR *ON SPEAKING TERMS*

AUDIO PROGRAM

The **Audio Program** was recorded in a way to provide learners with spoken samples that sound like real language. Learners will hear dysfluencies (reduced sounds, incomplete sentences, hesitations etc), simultaneous talk, interruptions, and so forth.

WEB MATERIALS

The web materials will contain instructor notes and assessment quizzes to accompany each chapter of the text. Instructor notes will explain the rationale behind the activities and provide simple and easy-to-understand explanations based on studies on language teaching and learning.

These materials will provide instructors with sound pedagogical explanations and help them develop as professionals.

By focusing on the real aspects of listening, speaking, and grammar, ***On Speaking Terms*** helps learners function in the community where they live, work, and learn.

Eliana Santana-Williamson
Yvonne Cranmer

CHAPTER

1 How Often Do You Do That?

GET STARTED

ACTIVITY A Listen to the shoppers as they each purchase an item. Write each conversation number below its corresponding picture.

CD 1 Track 1

a. ____________________

c. ____________________

b. ____________________

d. ____________________

ACTIVITY B Listen to the four conversations from Activity A again. Where are the customers in each conversation? What are they buying?

CD 1 Track 2

1. Where? ____________________ What? ____________________
2. Where? ____________________ What? ____________________
3. Where? ____________________ What? ____________________
4. Where? ____________________ What? ____________________

ACTIVITY **C** **1.** Match each picture with the correct location from the box below.

hardware store	department store	garage sale
farmers' market	college bookstore	

a. ____________ **b.** ____________ **c.** ____________

d. ____________ **e.** ____________

CD 1 Track 3

2. Listen to two speakers as they check their answers. Then check your answers with a partner. Refer to the Useful Expressions below to help you.

Useful
Expressions

"Hardware store" is letter . . . What do you think?

That's right/You're right. I agree.

I don't think so. I think "garage sale" is letter . . .

No way!

LEARN AND PRACTICE

GRAMMAR

Simple Present Tense and Adverbs of Frequency

You can use adverbs of frequency with the simple present tense to talk about habits and routines. One-word adverbs of frequency are usually placed between the subject and the verb.

Examples of one-word adverbs of frequency include *always*, *usually*, *often*, *rarely*, and *never*.

Two-word adverbs and longer adverb phrases are placed at the end of the sentence.

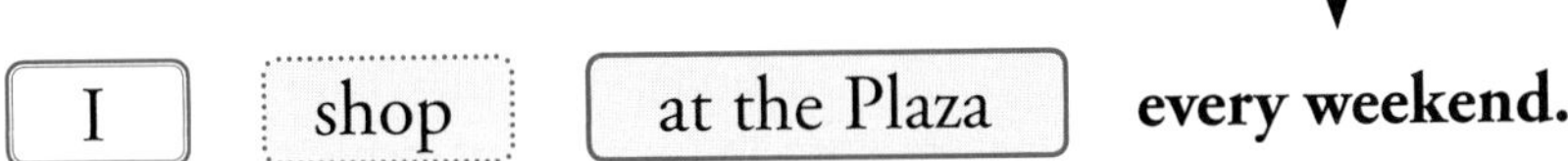

Examples of two-word adverbs and longer adverb phrases include the following:

once a . . . **twice a . . .** **every other . . .** **every . . .**	**day, week, month, year**

To form a *yes/no* question with an adverb of frequency, insert *do* at the beginning of the sentence.

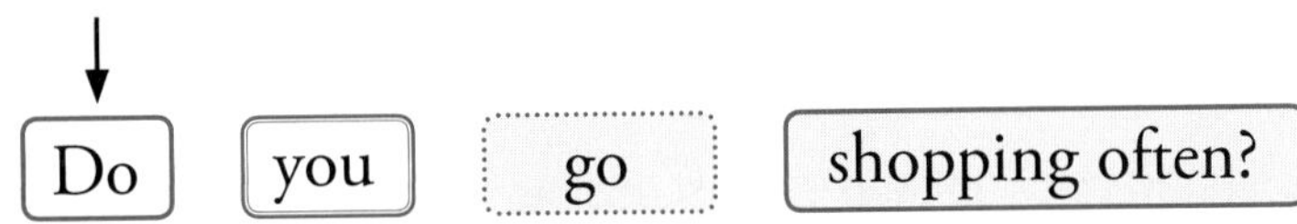

Affirmative Answers		Negative Answers	
Yes, I do.	Uh-huh.	No, I don't.	No, not really.
Yes, I love shopping.	Yep.	I don't like shopping.	Nope.

(continued)

GRAMMAR (*continued*)

If you want to ask a *How often* question, insert a *How often* before *do*.

How often | do | you | go | shopping?

To answer a *How often* question, your answer does not always need to be a complete sentence. You can answer using only the adverb of frequency.

For example: **A:** How often do you go shopping?
B: Once a month. I don't like shopping very much.

ACTIVITY **A** Instructor Demo

CD 1 Track 4

1. Listen to a group of students trying to find out as much as possible about their instructor's routine and habits.
2. As a class, try to find out as much as possible about your instructor's routine and habits. Ask *yes/no* questions, *how often* questions, and other questions with *wh-* pronouns. Be sure to include adverbs of frequency in your questions.

ACTIVITY **B**

1. Fill in the chart below with places where you frequently go shopping, who you go with, how often you go, and the reasons why you go there.

Where	With	How Often	Why
yard sales or garage sales	my husband	every other Saturday	to look for things for our new house

CD 1 Track 5

2. Listen to two speakers discussing their answers to the chart.
3. Now, work with a partner. Find out where your partner goes shopping, who he or she goes with, how often, and why. Listen for the adverbs of frequency that your partner uses.

SPEAKING STRATEGIES

Speaking versus Writing: Special Strategies for Conversations

Many features of speaking are not common in writing. It is important to see that speaking is not as "neat" or "perfect" as we may think. Speakers use many different strategies to help them gain time to think while talking, to modify what they are saying, to ask for clarification when they don't understand, and so on.

ACTIVITY **C** **1.** Read the two examples below. One of the examples is a written text, and the other example is a conversation.

Example 1	Example 2
Mom, I stopped by to see you today, but you weren't home! So, I'm writing this note for you. Guess what? Last weekend, I went to the new shopping mall on Route 1. Everything is on sale this month. We have to go there together! Do you want to go out this weekend to do some shopping with me? Call me when you get home so we can make plans. We've got to go! Love, Amber	**A:** Mom? Did you just get home? **B:** Hi, Sweetie. Yes, I did. How are you doing? **A:** Great! Hey, Mom, I went shopping last weekend at the new shopping mall on, um, on Route 1. **B:** Oh, really? Oh, yes . . . I see your note right here. **A:** Yeah, it was great! They have, they have all these stores and, uh . . . well, everything was on sale . . . **B:** That's good! **A:** Yeah! So, uh . . .do you, do you wanna go out next weekend . . . to do some shopping with me, Mom? **B:** Sure . . . I'd love to. **A:** All right, then. Uh, ten, ten o'clock . . . on Saturday? **B:** Sounds great! **A:** All right, I've gotta go now. See you on Saturday, then. **B:** OK, Sweetie. Love you. **A:** Love you, too. Bye. **B:** Bye.

Wanna is a reduced form of *want to* and is very common in conversational American English.

Gotta or *I've gotta* are very common phrases used in conversation. Speakers often drop the word *have* before *gotta.*

2. Discuss the differences between the written text and the conversation above with a partner. Write the key differences on the lines below. Refer to the Useful Expressions on the next page to help you discuss these texts.

____

____

____

____

____

Useful
Expressions

In Example 1, . . .	Also, . . .
Example 2 has no . . .	Anything else?

CD 1 Track 6

3. Listen to two speakers discussing the differences in the examples. As you listen, check your answers.

LISTENING AND SPEAKING STRATEGIES

Asking for Repetition

When you write, you have time to think about what you want to say and how you want to say it. When you speak, you don't have time to plan what to say or how to say it. Occasionally, speakers don't understand or hear what another speaker has said, so they use speaking strategies to help them get the information. Below you will learn the strategy called *asking for repetition.*

Look at the expressions we can use to ask for repetition in an informal way:

- What?
- Huh?
- Yeah?

You can use these expressions in informal situations with close friends or family members. When using these informal expressions, pay careful attention to your tone. In some situations, using these informal expressions to ask for repetition can sound rude.

Look at the expressions we can use to ask for repetition in a more formal way:

- Sorry?
- Excuse me? OR 'Scuse me?
- Beg your pardon? Pardon?
- Repeat a key phrase from the sentence. For example:

  A: Who is your favorite actress?
  B: Um . . . my favorite actress? Oh . . . Julia Roberts.

These expressions and strategies are used when we are in a more formal situation. For example, they are used while at work, at school, or when talking to a boss or professor. They are considered to be more polite than the informal expressions above.

If you listen for these expressions and phrases during a conversation, you can often determine if a conversation is formal or informal.

ACTIVITY **D** Read the conversation below. The customer and salesperson are at a clothing store in the mall. There is loud music playing. Circle the ways that the speakers ask for repetition.

Salesperson: Hi, there. May I help you find something?
Customer: Oh, um . . . yeah, actually I'm looking for a jean skirt.
Salesperson: Pardon? Jean . . . ? There is a lot of noise. I can't hear you very well.
Customer: Jean skirt.
Salesperson: OK, well, we have, we have many in stock.
Customer: Um, you don't have any?
Salesperson: No, we have *many* in stock. They're right over here. Would you like me to show you?
Customer: Excuse me?
Salesperson: I'll show them to you.
Customer: Oh, thanks!

ACTIVITY **E** CD 1 Track 7 Listen to the four parts of a conversation. One speaker is asking the other speaker to repeat some information. Write the phrases that the speaker uses to ask for repetition.

Part 1: ____________________
Part 2: ____________________
Part 3: ____________________
Part 4: ____________________

ACTIVITY **F** CD 1 Track 8 Listen to the conversation again. Decide how formal you think the conversation is and mark it on the scale below. Discuss your answer with the class. Give examples from the conversation to explain why you chose that answer.

(very informal) 1 – 2 – 3 – 4 – 5 (very formal)

Cultural Note It is important to determine how formal a conversation should be when we are speaking. If we speak too informally, the people we are talking to may think that we are impolite. If we are speaking with friends, we can speak informally. In a more formal situation, it is important to use more formal speaking strategies and ask people for repetition politely.

1. Listen to two students talking about their hobbies, habits, and characteristics.
2. Look at the chart below. Go around the classroom and try to find classmates who have the hobbies, habits, and characteristics listed in the chart. When you don't understand what someone says, ask for repetition using the strategies from page 6. Refer to the Useful Expressions below to help you to react to your classmates' responses.

Find someone who . . .	Name
• has an unusual pet.	
• goes to bed after midnight.	
• studies every day.	
• has more than two siblings.	
• hates watching TV.	
• loves to read.	
• has a unique hobby.	
• plays the piano.	

Useful
Expressions

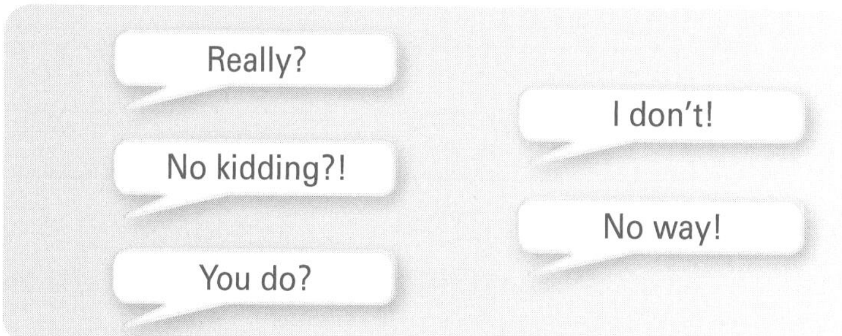

Really?
No kidding?!
You do?
I don't!
No way!

GRAMMAR

Using Collocations

Just like magnets, some words are attracted to one another. For example, in English we say *do homework*, not *make homework*; we *make a cake*, not *do a cake*. These pairs of words are used together regularly and are called collocations. In different languages, words collocate differently. For example, it's common to hear Spanish speakers say *take lunch*; however, in English, *lunch* collocates with *have* or *eat* rather than *take*. Likewise, we *dye our hair* but we *paint the walls*, even though we are changing the color of something in both instances.

ACTIVITY **H** Find the mistakes in the collocations below and correct them with a partner. Refer to the Useful Expressions to help you with your discussion.

> The verbs *make, get, give,* and *take* are very frequent in conversational English.

a. take breakfast

b. do the bed

c. say a lie

d. make a test

e. take a driver's license

Useful
Expressions

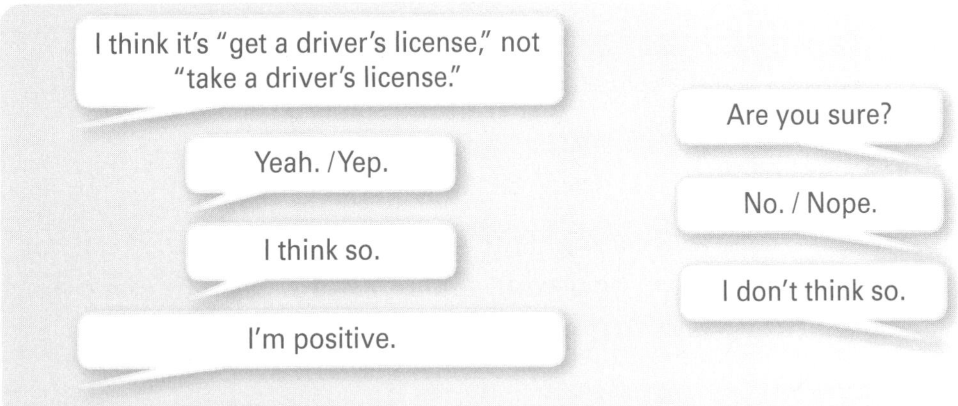

I think it's "get a driver's license," not "take a driver's license."
Are you sure?
Yeah. / Yep.
No. / Nope.
I think so.
I don't think so.
I'm positive.

ACTIVITY **I**
CD 1 Track 10

1. Listen to two speakers as they match the verbs with the correct phrases to complete the collocation.
2. Work with a partner. The column on the left contains verbs. The column on the right has noun phrases. Match the verbs on the left to the phrases on the right to complete a collocation. You can use a verb more than once. Refer to the Useful Expressions on the next page as you discuss your answers. Ask your instructor for help when you do not know how to say something.

Verbs	Phrases
do the laundry	the bed
have breakfast, a ride	a ride
get an I.D, a ride	the laundry
give ice cream, a sandwich	someone home
take a test, someone home	breakfast
eat a sandwich	a sandwich
make the bed	ice cream
	an I.D.
	a test

Useful
Expressions

What can you "do"?

What about "take"?

Yeah. That's right.

You "do the laundry" . . .

I don't think you can say "take breakfast."

I'm pretty sure.

I'm not sure.

GRAMMAR

Collocations with *Get* and *Go*

The verbs *get* and *go* are among the most common verbs used in conversational English. *Get* and *go* can be used in different ways with different words. Look at the examples of words that collocate with *get* and *go*:

Get	Go
get a cold	**go** shopping
get going	**go** somewhere
get something	**go** crazy
get angry	**go** ahead

ACTIVITY **J** Complete the conversation with *get* or *go*.

A: Hi, Honey. Do you wanna ________ (a) something to eat?

B: Not hungry.

A: Really? Well, then, we uh . . . we could ________ (b) window-shopping.

B: I don't have any money.

A: Oh, come on! Let's ________ (c) somewhere. I'm bored!

B: Oh, OK. Where?

A: Let's ________ (d) a pizza.

B: All right, then. Can you just wait ten minutes?

A: Oh, come on! Let's ________ (e) going.

ACTIVITY **K** Work in groups of three. Choose one person to be the secretary. The secretary will write down your group's answers. Your instructor will choose a verb from the box below. Your group will have two minutes to think of as many words that collocate with that verb as possible. The group with the most correct collocations wins. Refer to the example below before you begin.

work	go	come	say
help	clean	make	prepare
call	take	watch	eat

Example

Collocations
work out at the gym
work on homework

PRONUNCIATION

Rising and Falling Intonation

Intonation is the way your voice goes higher and lower when you speak. Intonation is important because it can change the meaning of what you say.

Rising intonation is represented by the symbol (↑). It is used when you ask for repetition and when you ask *Yes/No* questions. Your voice should go higher at the end of your sentence. For example: Excuse me? (↑)

Falling intonation is represented by the symbol (↓). It is used when giving an answer or making a statement. Your voice drops at the end of the sentence. For example: I said *five*. (↓)

CD 1 Track 11 Listen to the conversation. Look at the arrows for rising or falling intonation and repeat after the speakers.

A: Now, can I have your address? (↑)
B: Excuse me? (↑)
A: Your address. (↓)
B: Oh, . . . it's 1400 Prospector Boulevard. (↓)
A: Can you spell that? (↑)

CD 1 Track 12

Listen to the conversations below. Listen for how the speakers are using intonation. Then circle the arrow for rising intonation (↑) or the arrow for falling intonation (↓).

Conversation 1: **At a Swap Meet**

A:	I'd like to buy this picture.	(↑)	(↓)
B:	Excuse me?	(↑)	(↓)
A:	I want to get this picture.	(↑)	(↓)
B:	Oh, sorry. It's loud out here. Everything on that table is ten dollars.	(↑)	(↓)
A:	Fine. Can I give you a 50-dollar bill?	(↑)	(↓)
B:	Um, do you have something smaller?	(↑)	(↓)
A:	Uh . . . let me see. Um . . . can I give you a twenty?	(↑)	(↓)
B:	Oh. OK, sure. I have change for a twenty.	(↑)	(↓)

Conversation 2: **In the Music Store at the Mall**

A:	You can get 30 percent off your purchase today if you sign up for our credit card. Do you want it?	(↑)	(↓)
B:	Oh, sure.	(↑)	(↓)
A:	All right. . . Could I have your name?	(↑)	(↓)
B:	Martin Luna. L-U-N-A.	(↑)	(↓)
A:	L-U-M-A?	(↑)	(↓)
B:	No, that's *n* like *Nancy,* not *m.*	(↑)	(↓)
A:	OK. And can I have your address please?	(↑)	(↓)
B:	1500 Palm Road. That's P-A-L-M. Austin, Texas, 78701.	(↑)	(↓)

Cultural Note

When people want to sell things they no longer need, they sometimes set up tables and try to sell their items themselves. This is called a yard sale or garage sale. A flea market (or swap meet) is similar to a yard sale, but is a place where a larger group of people gather to sell their goods. Garage sales and swap meets are places where you can get items for lower prices than you would pay if you bought the item at a store. Bargaining is often expected during these types of events. If you are buying an item from a regular store, it is not polite or acceptable to try and bargin for a different price.

ACTIVITY **M** Work with a partner. Sit facing each other and practice the conversations from Activity L. One person should be Speaker A and the other person should be Speaker B. Monitor your partner's use of rising and falling intonation.

SPEAKING STRATEGIES

Speaking Politely: Conversations with a Beginning, a Middle, and an End

Polite conversations generally have a sequence that includes a beginning, a middle, and an end. When we buy an item from a vendor, conversations usually include these parts:

Beginning: Opening Greeting

A: Hi there.
B: Good morning.

Middle: Purchasing an Item

A: I want to get/buy this . . . How much is it?	**Explain What you Want**
B: It's . . . dollars. Everything on the table is . . . All these are . . .	**Vendor Responds**
A: I'll give you 15 dollars for it.	**Customer Bargains**
B: Ok. Let me wrap it for you. How about 20? It's made of solid wood. Sorry, 25 is the final price.	**Vendor Accepts Offer or . . .** **Vendor Makes Counter Offer or . . .** **Vendor Rejects Offer**

End: Final Comments / Say Goodbye

A: Oh thanks. / Thanks anyway.
B: Have a nice day.
A: You too.

ACTIVITY **N** The conversations below are each broken into four parts. Put the conversations in order by placing 1, 2, 3 or 4 in the parentheses in each box. Then identify the part of the conversation and write it on the line in each box.

Conversation 1:

( ) ______________________

____

B: Thanks.
A: No problem. Have a good day.
B: You too.

( ) ______________________

____

A: Oh. I'll give you 35 for it.
B: Um . . . It's a really old and good clock. How about 40?
A: 38?
B: Um . . . Ok.
A: Great! Here it is.

(1) *Beginning: Opening Greeting*

A: Hi!
B: Hi there!
A: Let me know if you want something.
B: Sure.

( ) ______________________

____

A: Um, how much is this clock?
B: 50.
A: Pardon me?
B: Fifty.

Conversation 2:

( ) ______________________

____

A: Um, how much is this?
B: Only 75.
A: Oh.
B: It's a great table.

( ) ______________________

____

A: Uh-huh. I'll give you 55 for it.
B: I'm sorry. 75 is the final price
A: 70?
B: I'm sorry.

( ) ______________________

____

A: Good morning
B: Good morning.

( ) ______________________

____

A: OK. Thanks anyway.
B: No problem. Have a good day.
A: You too.

REVIEW AND EXPAND

ACTIVITY A
CD 1 Track 13

Listen to four conversations. Then discuss the questions below with a partner. If necessary, take brief notes on the lines below.

- How did the people ask for repetition?
- How much was the item?
- Did the person buy the item?

Conversation 1: ______________________________

____

____

Conversation 2: ______________________________

____

____

Conversation 3: ______________________________

____

____

Conversation 4: ______________________________

____

____

CD 1 Track 14

1. Listen to two of the conversations again. Mark each line with an up arrow (↑) for rising intonation or a down arrow (↓) for falling intonation.

Conversation 1	Conversation 2
A: Hi. I want to buy this black dress. How much is it?	**A:** Excuse me? How much is this?
B: It's 25 dollars.	**B:** It's 30 dollars.
A: Twenty-five dollars?	**A:** 'Scuse me. Thirteen?
B: Yes.	**B:** No, thir-ty.
A: I'll give you 15.	**A:** How about 20?
B: Oh, I'm sorry. It's not negotiable.	**B:** Um . . . 20?
A: OK. Too bad.	**A:** Mm-hmm.
	B: Well, all right. Twenty it is.
	A: Great. I'll take it.

2. Work with a partner and compare your answers.

ACTIVITY **C** **1.** Imagine that you are at a swap meet or garage sale. Half of the class will be selling their items. The other half of the class will be customers. The sellers should decide upon and write an asking price for each item in the chart below.

Item	Asking Price (Sellers)	Purchase Price (Customers)
an old silver ring, size 10	$	$
a handmade sweater, medium		
a painting of the ocean		
a bicycle		
a black leather jacket, large		
a pink ceramic vase		
a gold watch, broken		
an English dictionary		

2. Each customer has $30.00 to spend and must purchase four items. Customers should approach a seller, ask for the price of an item, bargain with the seller, and decide if they are going to buy the item. Customers should speak with different sellers to try and get the best bargain on each item. Customers should write down the price they pay for each item in the chart above. Refer to the Useful Expressions below to help your discussion.

Useful ***Expressions***

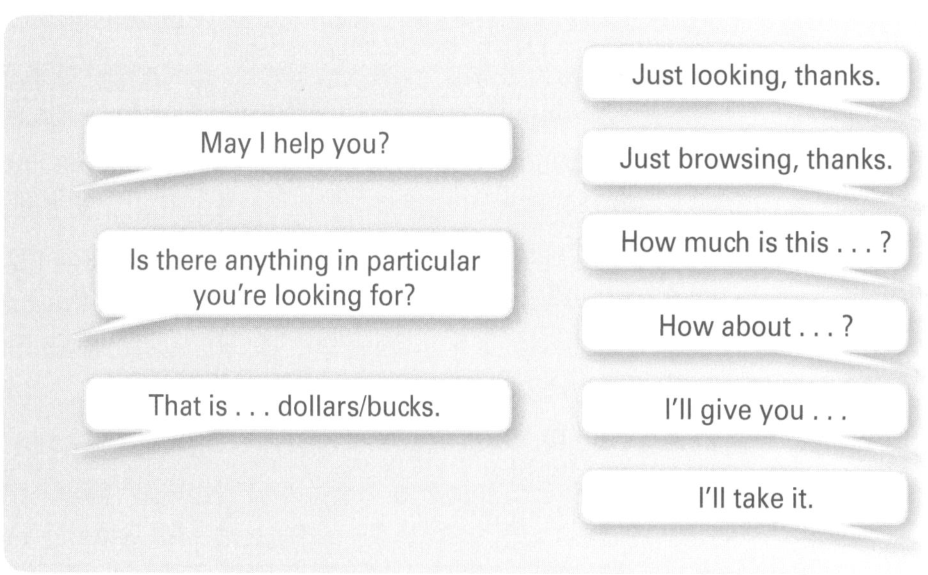

May I help you?
Is there anything in particular you're looking for?
That is . . . dollars/bucks.
Just looking, thanks.
Just browsing, thanks.
How much is this . . . ?
How about . . . ?
I'll give you . . .
I'll take it.

3. Students should switch roles—customers become the sellers, sellers become the customers—and repeat the activity.

ACTIVITY D
CD 1 Track 15

1. Listen to two speakers discussing the items they purchased at the garage sale in Activity C.
2. Work with a partner. Discuss the items that you bought and how much you paid for each item. Refer to the Useful Expressions below to help you.

Useful ***Expressions***

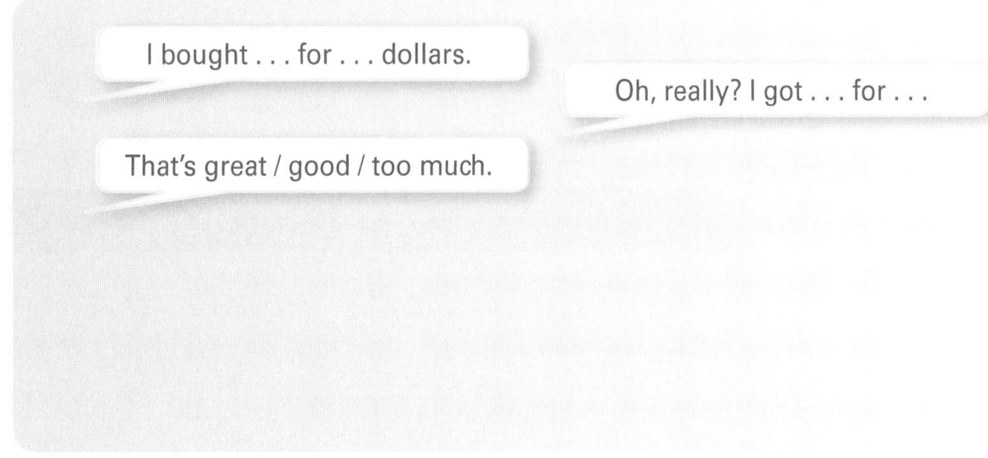

I bought . . . for . . . dollars.
Oh, really? I got . . . for . . .
That's great / good / too much.

Got is the past tense form of *get.* In this context, it means *bought. Got* is informal.

EVALUATION

ACTIVITY A

Now that you have completed the activities in this chapter, complete the self-evaluation checklist below. Discuss your checklist with a classmate.

Self-Evaluation Checklist

- ☐ I used the simple present tense and adverbs of frequency correctly.
- ☐ I was able to use collocations correctly.
- ☐ I asked for repetition when I didn't understand.
- ☐ I was sure that my conversations included a beginning, a middle, and an end.
- ☐ I used rising intonation and falling intonation properly.

ACTIVITY **B** Look back at the chapter and the self-evaluation checklist above. What can you do this week to improve the skills you have learned in this chapter? Talk with a partner and write an action plan for how you can improve your skills this week.

Example I need to work on using rising intonation when I ask for repetition. Every time I speak English, I'm going to focus on this. I need more practice with adverbs of frequency and I will review how to use adverbs of frequency with the simple present tense.

Action Plan

CHAPTER

2 | Where Can I Find That?

GET STARTED

CD 1 Track 16

Listen to three conversations. Each conversation is taking place in a different location. Write the conversation number below the corresponding picture.

a. ________________ b. ________________ c. ________________

CD 1 Track 17

1. Listen to two speakers discuss the methods used in their countries to get someone's attention.
2. Work with a partner. Discuss how to get someone's attention in your country. Refer to the questions and the Useful Expressions to help you with your discussion.

How do you get someone's attention . . .

- in a restaurant? (a waiter or server; someone at another table)
- in the hall at school? (your friend; your instructor; your boss)
- on the street? (your friend; a stranger)

Useful
Expressions

In my country, we say . . .

It's very rude to . . . , but it's OK to . . .

It's polite to say . . . to your instructor.

It's OK to say . . . to your friend.

Really? In my country, we . . . , but not in a nice restaurant.

LEARN AND PRACTICE

SPEAKING STRATEGIES

Getting Someone's Attention

We use different expressions to get people's attention. Sometimes, expressions that are considered polite in one situation may be considered rude in another. Consequently, it is important to learn both informal and formal expressions to get someone's attention. Look at the examples below.

Hi, there. (informal)

'Scuse me. (informal)

Pardon me. (formal)

Excuse me. (formal)

Hello. (formal or informal)

ACTIVITY **A** Half of the class will be in Group A and the other half will be in Group B. Students in both groups will walk around the classroom. Each student in Group B will get the attention of a student in Group A and then ask for the time. Students in Group B should ask three people for the time. Then students in each group should switch roles. Refer to the Useful Expressions below to help you and remember to ask for repetition when necessary.

Useful ***Expressions***

What time is it, please?

Do you have the time?

Sorry, I don't have the time.

REVIEW: SPEAKING STRATEGIES

Asking for Repetition

When we speak with another person, we sometimes don't quite understand what the other person is saying. In order to get all of the information, it is important to learn how to ask for repetition. Review the examples of how to ask for repetition.

Informal	Formal
• What? • Huh? • Yeah?	• Sorry? • Excuse me? OR 'Scuse me? • Beg your pardon? Pardon? • Repeating the sentence.

CD 1 Track 18

Listen to two conversations and circle the correct answer to each question. For some questions, more than one answer is possible.

Conversation 1: A customer is in a bookstore. He wants to buy a box of computer disks.

1. What did the customer say to get the attention of the clerk?

a. 'Scuse me. c. Sorry.

b. Hey. d. Hello!

2. What two things did the clerk say to ask for repetition? (Circle two answers.)

a. Computer disks? c. What?

b. Pardon? d. The clerk repeated the customer's sentence.

Conversation 2: A student goes to the campus bookstore to get a book she ordered.

3. What did the customer say to get the attention of the clerk?

a. 'Scuse me. c. Sorry.

b. Hey. d. Pardon me.

4. How did the clerk ask for repetition?

a. 553-26-123 what? c. What?

b. Pardon? d. The clerk repeated the customer's sentence.

ACTIVITY C Work with a partner. Ask your partner questions and complete the form below. When you don't understand what he or she says, ask for repetition politely.

Personal Information

Name: ______________ Date of birth: ______________

Married: ______________ Single: ______________

Children: Y ________ N ________ Number of children: ________

Telephone number: ______________________________

Three likes: ______________________________

____

____

Three dislikes: ______________________________

____

____

Future plans: ______________________________

LISTENING STRATEGIES

Asking for and Following Directions

Sometimes you may need to find a specific item in places such as a grocery store, bookstore, pharmacy, and so on. When you need to locate an item, you must be able to ask for, listen to, and understand directions. When asking for directions, you should do the following:

- Get someone's attention. ⟶ Excuse me. / Hello. / Pardon me.
- Ask where something is located. ⟶ Where can I find . . . ? / Where is the . . . ?
- Repeat the directions. ⟶ OK, on Aisle 3. / So, it's at the back of the store.
- Say *thank you.*

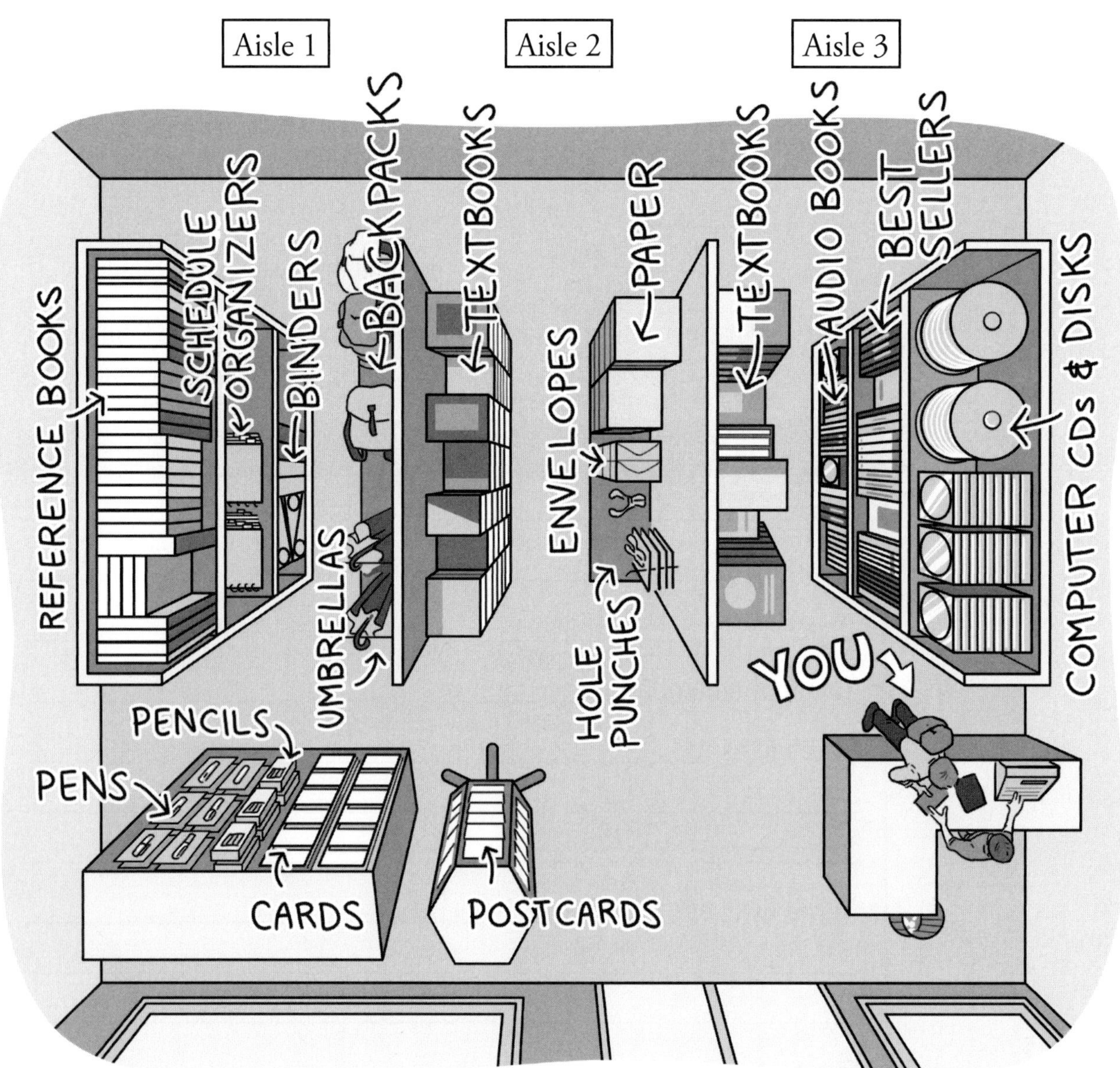

 ACTIVITY D
CD 1 Track 19

Look at the bookstore map on page 22 and listen to a clerk giving directions. Follow the clerk's directions and locate the item on the store map. What item is the clerk directing the customer to? Write down each item and then listen for the answer.

Directions	What item do you see?
1. Go down the far right aisle. Look right. They're on the top shelf.	*computer CDs*
2. Go down Aisle 2. Look on the left on the bottom shelf.	___
3. Go to the middle aisle. Look on the right.	___
4. Go down Aisle 1. They're on the left on the middle shelf.	___
5. Go down the far left aisle to the back of the store. They're on the top left shelf.	___

ACTIVITY E

Pretend you are a clerk in a bookstore. A customer is asking you to help her locate a specific item. Choose three of the items in the box below. Look at the map of the bookstore on page 22 and locate each item. Write directions for each item on the lines below.

backpacks	pens and pencils	umbrellas
envelopes	audio books	binders
bestsellers	postcards	paper

1. **Item:** ___

   Directions: ___

2. **Item:** ___

   Directions: ___

3. **Item:** ___

   Directions: ___

ACTIVITY **F** 1. Work with a partner. Choose a type of store that this interaction will take place in (do not choose a bookstore). One student is a store clerk. The other student is a customer who is looking for a particular item. Follow the prompts in the boxes below and create a conversation with your partner. Refer to the example conversation below to help you. Do not write the conversation down.

Customer

- Get the clerk's attention.
- Ask where something is.
- Repeat the directions.
- Say *thank you.*

Clerk

- Ask for repetition.
- Give directions.
- Correct directions.

Example

Customer: Hello.

Clerk: Hi.

Customer: Where are the tennis rackets, please?

Clerk: Pardon me?

Customer: The tennis rackets?

Clerk: Oh, um . . . go down the left aisle over there. They're on the right near the . . . the . . . rollerblades.

Customer: OK. So, go down the left aisle, and they're on the right.

Clerk: Yes.

Customer: Thanks.

2. Stand up and act out your conversation for the class. Use all of the speaking strategies you have learned to help you communicate. The class should listen to each conversation and try to guess what type of store the conversation is taking place in.

GRAMMAR

Using Modals to Ask for Personal Information

There are different ways to ask for personal information politely. One way to ask for information politely is by using modal verbs such as *can*, *could*, and *may*. Modals are very common in conversation and are often used to ask for personal information during transactions. The most common modal for asking for information is *can*. Look at the examples below.

Can	I	have	your name, please?
Could	I	see	your ID?
May	I	have	your e-mail address?

ACTIVITY G
CD 1 Track 20

Listen to the admissions office clerk ask for the students' names and personal information. Complete the questions with the modals you hear.

Conversation 1:

a. ________________ I help you?

b. ________________ I have your name, please?

c. ________________ you spell that, please?

d. ________________ I have your student ID?

Conversation 2:

e. ________________ I have your name, please?

f. ________________ I have your student number?

Conversation 3:

g. How ________________ I help you?

h. ________________ I have your address?

ACTIVITY **H** What questions could the people below ask you when they are trying to learn your personal information? Write a question for each line below. Be sure to use a modal in your question.

a. A police officer: *Can I see your driver's license?* ______

b. A cashier at a bank: ______

c. A telephone salesperson: ______

d. The school registrar secretary: ______

ACTIVITY **I** Instructor Demo

CD 1 Track 21

1. Listen to the students as they try to guess what role their instructor is playing based on the modals she is using.

2. Your instructor will choose one of the roles from the list below. He or she will use modals to ask for your personal information. As a class, guess what role your instructor is playing.

Roles:

- bank cashier
- grocery store cashier
- nurse or doctor
- school counselor
- pharmacist
- school admissions clerk

3. Work in groups of four. One student should choose a role from the list above and use modals to ask their group members for personal information. The other members of the group have to guess what role the student is playing. The group member who guesses correctly chooses a new role and begins the exercise again.

ACTIVITY **J**
CD 1 Track 22

1. Listen to two students as they use modals to ask for personal information.

2. Work with a partner. Greet your partner and ask for his or her telephone number. Use *may*, *can*, or *could* in your questions. Your conversation should follow the steps below. Repeat the exercise with three more classmates.

1. Get your classmate's attention.
2. Ask for his or her name and introduce yourself if you don't know him or her.
3. Ask for his or her telephone number.
4. Ask for repetition when necessary.
5. Ask what time of day is best to call him or her.
6. Write the information down.
7. Thank him or her.

PRONUNCIATION

Intonation for *Yes/No* Questions with Modals

We use rising intonation at the end of *yes/no* questions. Questions starting with *may I*, *can I*, or *could I* are a type of *yes/no* question. As a result, we use rising intonation at the end of these questions. In other words, our voice goes higher because we are using a higher pitch.

CD 1 Track 23

Listen and repeat.

A police officer has stopped your car.

A: May I have your driver's license, Ma'am? (↑)

B: Yes, Officer. Um, let me see, here it is.

A: And could I see proof of insurance? (↑)

B: Yes. Here it is.

A: And can I have your registration? (↑)

B: Hold on a minute. OK. Here you go.

Cultural Note

Dealing with police officers and other law enforcement officials may differ from country to country. In the United States, if a police officer signals for you to stop your vehicle, you should pull over to the side of the road, put your hands on the steering wheel, and remain inside your vehicle until the police officer approaches you. The police officer will likely ask you for personal information, your driver's license, and proof of car insurance. You should greet the police officer politely and use formal language if possible.

 ACTIVITY K

CD 1 Track 24

1. Listen to the conversation and repeat after the speakers.
2. Work with a partner. On a separate sheet of paper, rewrite the conversation and change the underlined information to your own ideas. Practice your new conversation with your partner and monitor your partner's use of rising intonation.

A: I was wondering if you could help me. I want to see if my book is here yet.

B: What book?

A: I ordered a book for my grammar class. Is it here yet?

B: Could I have your name, please?

A: It's Yuki Fuwasaki. F-U-W-A-S-A-K-I.

B: Um, may I have your student number?

A: 553-26-1234.

REVIEW AND EXPAND

ACTIVITY A

1. Work in groups of three. Each group member should choose one of the following roles:

   Student 1: You are buying something in a bookstore.

   Student 2: You are a clerk at the bookstore.

   Student 3: You are a cashier at the bookstore.

2. With your group, create a conversation using the guidelines in the chart below. Use the map of the bookstore on page 22. Then switch roles and repeat the exercise.

Student 1	Student 2	Student 3
• Get the clerk's attention. • Ask where an item is. • Repeat the clerk's directions. • Find the item and go to the cashier.	• Ask for repetition. • Give directions. • Correct directions.	• Greet the student. • Ask for personal information. • Ask, "Will that be all?"

Will that be all? is often used in transactions. It means *"Do you want more?"* or *"Do you need anything else?"* Phrases like *"Will that be it?"* or *"All set?"* are also commonly used in transactions.

ACTIVITY **B**
CD 1 Track 25

1. Listen to a group of students role-playing a conversation between a clerk and customers in a store.
2. Work in groups of three. Choose one student in each group to be the clerk. The other group members are the customers. You are at a pharmacy (drugstore).

Student 1: The Clerk

Look at the map of the store on page 173. Look at the items on the list. Choose a location for each item on the list and draw it in the map. The customers will ask where certain items are located in the store. Look at your map and give the customers directions to each item.

Students 2 and 3: The Customers

Look at the list of items on page 174. Each customer is shopping for the items on his or her list. Each customer should get the clerk's attention politely and ask for the first item on their list. Customers need to follow directions, locate the item in the store, and write the name of the item in the correct location on the map. Compare your completed map with Student 1 to see if you correctly located the item.

EVALUATION

ACTIVITY **A** Now that you have completed the activities in this chapter, complete the self-evaluation checklist below. Discuss your checklist with a classmate.

Self-Evaluation Checklist

- ☐ I was able to get someone's attention politely.
- ☐ I asked for repetition when necessary.
- ☐ I asked for and followed directions without difficulty.
- ☐ I used modals to politely ask for personal information.
- ☐ I used rising intonation with modal verbs.

ACTIVITY **B** Look back at the chapter and the self-evaluation checklist above. What can you do this week to improve the skills you have learned in this chapter? Talk with a partner. Then, turn to the next page and write an action plan for how you can improve your skills this week.

Example I need to work on asking for personal information with modals. So, I'm going to make sure I use at least two modals, *can* and *may*, when I am asking someone for personal information. I also need to focus on using rising intonation correctly. I will listen to the audio to hear examples of rising intonation.

Action Plan

CHAPTER

3 | I'm a Very Healthy Person

GET STARTED

ACTIVITY A

CD 1 Track 26

Listen to the conversations. As you listen, close your eyes. Visualize where the speakers are and what they are doing. Listen again and write the conversation number below its corresponding picture.

a. ____________

c. ____________

b. ____________

d. ____________

ACTIVITY B

What was the topic of each conversation you just heard? Write the number of the correct conversation on the lines below.

Topic	**Conversation**
Exercising	________
Stress	________
Eating habits	________
Drinking soda	________

ACTIVITY C CD 1 Track 27

Listen to each conversation from Activity A again. What good habits and bad habits do you hear in each conversation? Write the good and bad habits in the chart below.

	Good Habits	Bad Habits
Conversation 1		
Conversation 2		
Conversation 3		
Conversation 4		

ACTIVITY D

Think about your own habits. Make a list of the good habits and the bad habits you have. Write your habits in the chart below.

Good Habits	Bad Habits
I wake up early.	*I watch too much TV.*
I exercise three times a week.	*I eat too much junk food.*

ACTIVITY E CD 1 Track 28

1. Listen to two students discussing what they have for breakfast.
2. Work in groups of four. Discuss your health habits with your group members. Which of your group members has the healthiest habits? Refer to the Useful Expressions on the next page to help your conversation.

Remember to . . .

- ask for repetition if you don't understand.
- ask your instructor for help if you don't know how to say something.

Useful
Expressions

Do you eat healthy food?

No, you don't!

Oh, I see.

That's bad for you, though.

Do you exercise?

You do?

Really? That's great!

Good for you!

LEARN AND PRACTICE

SPEAKING STRATEGIES

Real Speaking versus Writing

Some important differences exist between speaking and writing. When we write, we have time to plan, write our ideas down, and revise our work. When we speak, we have to think and talk at the same time. We often do not have time to think carefully about what we say or how we say it. We must quickly think about what we want to say, put the language together, and continue the conversation. In order to do all these things at the same time, we use speaking strategies to help us. Strategies for real speaking include the following:

1. We hesitate while we talk. We use sounds, we repeat words, or we simply pause.

   A: I, **I, um . . .** don't think that's a great idea!

2. We use incomplete sentences, or sentence parts, instead of complete sentences.

   A: What's your favorite color?

   B: **Yellow.**

3. We react to what people say with words or sounds.

   A: I work eight hours a day and go to school.

   B: **Whew!** That sounds like a lot!

4. Sometimes we speak at the same time as other people. This means that sometimes speech overlaps and we begin a new thought before the speaker has finished his or her thought.

   A: I do not know the answer to the question . . .

   B: I do! (Speaker B speaks at the same time as Speaker A)

   A: . . . in Activity A.

ACTIVITY **A** Read the texts below. Which one is more like real speaking? Which one is more like a written text? What are the differences? Discuss your answers with a partner.

Text 1	Text 2
A: Whew! Hey, Tim! What's up? **B:** Hey. **A:** How often do you use this treadmill? **B:** Oh, I'm . . . Five times a week. **A:** Oh, really? **B:** Yeah! **A:** Oh, boy, I'd like to do this more often, but you see I'm really . . . **B:** Uh, lazy? **A:** No, no. Now, see, I want to, but I'm just too . . . **B:** Uh, busy? **A:** That's it. **B:** Yeah. **A:** Too busy. You're right. **B:** Well . . . you know, exercising like this is really, really, good for your body and um . . . it's so good for your, you know, just your overall health. Your lung capacity, and it uses your major muscle groups. I love coming to the gym. **A:** Gee, I should do this a lot more often. **B:** Probably right.	**A:** Hey, Tim! What's up? **B:** Hey **A:** How often do you use this treadmill? **B:** I use it five times a week. **A:** That's great. **B:** Yes! **A:** I'd like to do this more often. **B:** Are you lazy? **A:** Not really. **B:** Are you busy? **A:** I'm pretty busy. **B:** Well, remember that when you exercise regularly, your heart and lungs are healthier. **A:** I know. **B:** So, what do you need to do? **A:** I know I need to get myself here more often.

SPEAKING STRATEGIES

Speak, Respond, React

During a conversation, it is very common for one speaker to comment on or react to what the other speaker is saying. Therefore, it is usual for conversations to have at least three steps: **speak, respond, react**.

(continued)

SPEAKING STRATEGIES (*continued*)

Speakers can continue their conversations simply by continuing to respond and react to one another.

Expressions for Reacting to a Conversation

When people react in a conversation, they often show their feelings or opinions. Reactions can show interest, agreement, contrasting opinion, and surprise. Study the reactions in the box below. Some expressions for reacting can show more than one feeling.

Interest	Agreement	Contrasting Opinion	Surprise
Really?	Yeah.	You do not!	Really?
Uh-huh.	You're right.	I don't think so.	Oh!
Oh?	Yes, I know what you mean.	I don't agree!	You're kidding?
You do?	Me, too.	Oh, I do!	No way!

ACTIVITY B Listen to four conversations. You will hear people react with interest, contrasting opinion, agreement, or surprise. Write the reactions you hear in the correct boxes below.

CD 1 Track 29

Interest	Agreement	Contrasting Opinion	Surprise

ACTIVITY C Read the conversation and write a reaction on the lines below. Be sure to write reactions that express interest, agreement, contrasting opinion, or surprise.

A: OK, my first question is . . .
B: Huh?
A: What's your favorite sport?
B: Soccer.
A: ______________________ (a)
B: Really?
A: Oh, yeah! I'm from Brazil!
B: Cool!
A: OK. Next question, um, wh-what's your favorite type of food?
B: I love sushi.
A: ______________________ (b) Now, um, . . . next. . . . What's your favorite TV show?
B: I hate TV.
A: ______________________ (c) You're the first person I ever talked to that hates TV.
B: Really?
A: Oh, yeah! Let's move on. Um . . . all right. . . Last question of the day . . .
B: OK.
A: What would you do if you won the lottery?
B: Oh, that's a good one. I'd quit my job.
A: ______________________ (d)

ACTIVITY D Write down five questions you want to ask your classmates. Work in groups of three. Ask your group members your questions and react to their answers.

1. ______________________
2. ______________________
3. ______________________
4. ______________________
5. ______________________

SPEAKING STRATEGIES

Sentence Parts

When speaking, we do not always use full sentences. We call these incomplete sentences *sentence parts.* When we speak, we do not usually need to worry about speaking in complete sentences.

CD 1 Track 30

Listen to the example.

Speaker 1:	Speaker 2:
(SPEAK) Uh, what are you eating? Do you always eat like that? So healthy.	**(RESPOND)** Yep. Very healthy.
(REACT) What else do you do to stay healthy?	**(RESPOND)** Exercise. I don't like it, but, you know . . .
(REACT) Really?	

Sentence Parts		Complete Sentences
So healthy.	=	Do you always eat so healthy?
Yep. Very healthy.	=	Yes, I always eat very healthy foods.
Exercise.	=	I also exercise.

ACTIVITY E Listen and write the sentence parts you hear.

CD 1 Track 31

A: I came to the U.S. when I was just 19.

B: ______________ (a)

A: Uh-huh. ______________ (b)

B: What did you do?

A: Well, I worked in a lot of different restaurants. You know, Chinese, American, places like that. I can speak a little Chinese.

B: ______________ (c) And what about your English?

A: ______________ (d) That's why I try to learn a few new words every day.

ACTIVITY **F** Look at the underlined sentence parts in the conversation below. As a class, discuss what the complete sentence would be for each sentence part.

Wanna is the reduced form of *want to.* It is often used in spoken English in informal situations.

A: How are you?

B: Fine, thanks. You?

A: I'm good. What are you doing?

B: Working on my homework assignment. You?

A: Me, too. Mine is due on Friday.

B: Wanna go to a party tonight?

A: Sorry. I have to work on my homework!

ACTIVITY **G**
CD 1 Track 32

1. Listen to two speakers ask and answer questions about their habits.
2. Work with a partner. Ask your partner the questions below. Your partner should answer each question with sentence parts only. Remember to react to his or her answers. Then switch roles and repeat the exercise.
   a. What time do you usually wake up?
   b. What do you have for breakfast?
   c. What do you usually have for lunch and dinner?
   d. What is your favorite food?
   e. Do you do any type of physical exercise?
   f. What kind of exercise do you do?
   g. How often do you exercise and where?

REVIEW: GRAMMAR

Simple Present Tense

When we talk about our habits, we use simple present tense. Simple present tense is also used to express likes and dislikes and to talk about people's physical features and families. Look at the examples below.

Affirmative Statements:

Habit:	I	make	my bed every day.
Likes/Dislikes:	I	like	to study.
Physical Features:	I	have	curly hair.
Family:	I	have	five brothers and sisters.

(continued)

REVIEW: GRAMMAR (*continued*)

Negative Statements:

I | do | not | wake up | at six during the week.

I | don't | like | to get up at six during the week.

***Yes/No* Questions:**

Do | you | make | your bed?

Do | you | have | a hobby ?

***Wh-* Questions:**

What time | do | you | go | to school?

How often | do | you | study?

ACTIVITY **H** Work with a partner. Discuss your good habits and your bad habits. Try to form affirmative statements, negative statements, *yes/no* questions, and *wh-* questions in the simple present tense. Refer back to the examples if you need help. Remember to respond and react to what your partner is saying.

ACTIVITY **I** **1.** Use the simple present tense and prepare five statements to say about yourself. One of the statements should be false. Write your statements in the box below.

Remember: One of your statements needs to be a lie!

1. Statement about your family: ______________________________
   (number of brothers and sisters, where they live, how old they are, etc.)
2. Statement about your schedule: ______________________________
   (what time you wake up, what time you exercise, study, eat dinner, etc.)
3. Statement about your shopping habits: ______________________________
   (how well you like shopping, where you shop, what store you like best, etc.)
4. Statement about what you like or don't like: ______________________________
   (what hobbies you like, what music or TV shows you like, what sports you enjoy playing, etc.)
5. Statement about the places you like to visit: ______________________________
   (what cities or countries you like to visit, what place you want to go to in the future, etc.)

CD 1 Track 33

2. Listen to a group of students playing a game. One student is explaining his list to the group and the group members are trying to guess which statement is false.

3. Work in groups of four or five. One student in each group starts by telling the group the statements he or she has written. The other group members will ask *yes/no* questions and try to guess the lie. For example, "Do you really exercise five days a week?" Remember, you need to use rising intonation when you ask *yes/no* questions. Refer to the Useful Expressions below to help your discussion.

4. Repeat the exercise so each member of the group has a chance to present his or her list of statements. The student who correctly guesses the most number of lies is the winner.

Useful *Expressions*

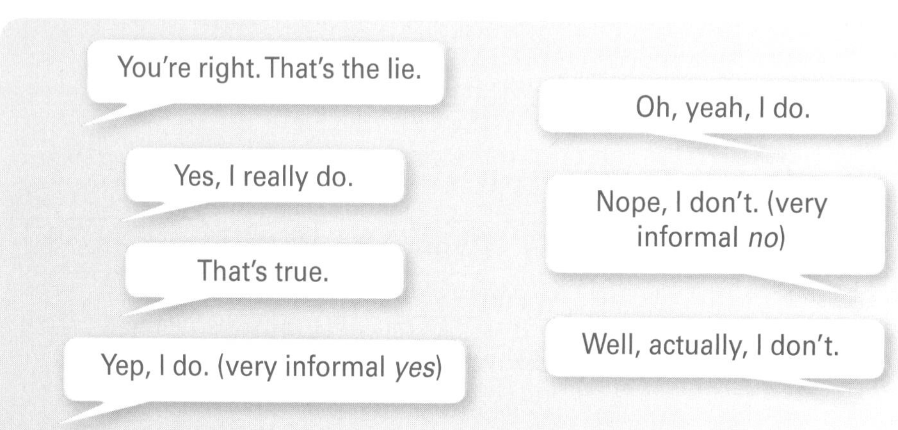

You're right. That's the lie.
Oh, yeah, I do.
Yes, I really do.
Nope, I don't. (very informal *no*)
That's true.
Well, actually, I don't.
Yep, I do. (very informal *yes*)

People sometimes use *actually* when they say something that might be a surprise to others.

ACTIVITY **J** Review the reactions for showing interest, agreement, a contrasting opinion, or surprise on page 35. What other expressions can you use to react to what someone says? Add more expressions to the box below.

Interest	Agreement	Contrasting Opinion	Surprise
Really?	Yes, I know what you mean.	I don't think so.	Really!
Cool!	Me too.	I don't!	You're kidding!
______	______	______	______
______	______	______	______
______	______	______	______

Cool is used in informal situations and means good or interesting.

GRAMMAR

Simple Present Tense and Third-Person Singular

We can use simple present tense and third-person singluar to talk about the habits of other people. The form of the simple present tense changes when we talk about someone else (*he* or *she*) or something (*it*) else.

In affirmative statements, we add an *s* to the verb:

She **loves** to watch television.

In negative statements, we use *doesn't* instead of *don't*:

I don't watch television.

She doesn't watch television.

In *yes/no* questions, we use *does* instead of *do*:

Does she love to watch television?

To form a *wh-* question using the third-person singular, we add a *wh-* word before *does*:

What time does she watch television?

ACTIVITY K Instructor Demo

CD 1 Track 34

1. Listen to a group of students playing the game "Guess Who I Am Thinking About."
2. Your instructor will choose a person that her or she knows well. You have to guess who this person is (a friend, a sibling, a parent, etc.) by asking as many *yes/no* questions as you can in five minutes. Remember to use simple present tense and the third-person singular in your questions.

GRAMMAR

Simple Present Tense: Asking Negative Questions

Negative questions are often used to find out if something you believe is true. For example:

You think your friend likes french fries. Now she says she does not like them. You might ask:

Don't | you | like | french fries?

Or you think your friend gets (understands) a joke you have told, but she doesn't laugh. You can ask:

Don't | you | get | it?

You can add a *wh-* question word (*who, what, when, where, why,* and *how*) to ask for further explanation.

Why | don't | you | get | it?

You can also add a person or a pronoun (*he, she,* or *it*) to ask for information about others. For example:

Doesn't | your mom | teach | at Green Elementary?

Doesn't | she | go | crazy with all the noise?

ACTIVITY **L** First, read the conversation below. Then complete the conversation with your own negative questions.

A: Are you ready . . . are you ready to go to the school picnic?

B: Well, um, . . . maybe.

A: ______________________________ (a)

B: Nope. I don't really want to go.

A: ______________________________ (b)

B: Well . . . no, um, I don't really like picnics much.

A: ______________________________ (c)

B: Nope. I really don't want to see all of our classmates.

A: ______________________________
(d)

B: Nooo. Barbecued hamburgers and hot dogs are bad for you. There's no way I'm going to go.

A: ______________________________
(e)

B: No, I don't get it at all. You wanted to go yesterday!

GRAMMAR

Simple Present Tense: Answering Negative Questions

When you answer negative questions, there are certain key parts of the question that will help you answer correctly. Do not pay attention to *don't* (the negative part of the sentence). Instead, pay attention to the main part of the question—the verb and other key words. If the main part of the question is true, answer *yes*. If the main part of the question is false, answer *no*.

For example:

Question	Main Part	True or False?	Answer
Don't you eat meat?	You eat meat?	True.	Yes. (I eat meat.)
		False.	No. (I don't eat meat).
Don't you have a son?	You have a son?	True.	Yes. (I have a son.)
		False.	No. (I don't have son.)

CD 1 Track 35

1. Listen to two speakers asking and answering negative questions.
2. Work in pairs with someone you know. Both of you will find out if something you believe about the other is true. On a separate sheet of paper, write down four negative questions. Then ask your partner the questions. Your partner has to answer those questions. Remember that these are *yes/no* questions, so you need to use rising intonation. Remember to follow these steps in your conversation: speak, respond, react.

Sentence Stress

Many students feel that native speakers of English speak too fast. However, the problem is not that English is spoken too fast. The problem is that some words are not pronounced exactly they way they are written. When we speak English, some words are stressed and others are reduced.

The words we stress are the most important words, or content words, in the sentence. Look at this sentence:

Would you like to see a movie tomorrow afternoon?

The most important words are the ones that carry meaning. If you delete the other ones, you can still understand the message. In the example above, the most important words (content words) are

. . . like . . . see . . . movie . . . tomorrow afternoon

The other words do not carry meaning. Look at these words below. If you hear only these words, you will not understand the meaning of the sentence.

Would you . . . to . . . a . . .

Therefore, the most important words (content words) are *stressed.*

Stressing Words in Sentences

To stress words in sentences:

1. Make the vowel sound longer.

2. Make your voice a little higher in pitch.

Listen to your instructor read this sentence as he or she emphasizes the important words:

Your homework is due on the first. Don't be late.

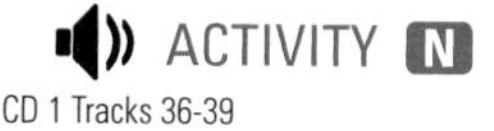

CD 1 Tracks 36-39

1. Listen to the first conversation line-by-line. Pay attention to the sentence stress on the underlined words. Then listen again and repeat each line after the speaker.

Conversation 1:

A: Hey, John! What's up with you today?

B: Nothing special. I see you're eating a sub today.

A: Yeah. I like to eat subs and things like that . . . healthy subs with lots of vegetables.

B: Good for you!

CD 1 Track 40

2. Now read the second conversation. Underline the words or syllables you think are stressed. Then listen and check your answers.

Conversation 2:

A: Hello, Lori. How are you today?
B: Well, I don't feel too well. I think I have the flu.
A: Don't you want to go see a doctor?
B: No, I don't want to go anywhere or see anyone.
A: Don't you want to go home and take a little nap?
B: No, I don't want to go anywhere or do anything.
A: Don't you want me to help you somehow?
B: Yeah. You can do my really difficult English homework for me.

3. Now, work with a partner. Sit facing each other. Practice the conversation above. Monitor your partner and be sure that he or she is correctly stressing the content words.

REVIEW AND EXPAND

ACTIVITY **A**

1. You want to find someone to be your roommate. Write on the lines below characteristics and habits that you don't like in a roommate. Remember to write your negative statements in the simple present tense.

I don't want a roomate who . . .

1. is disorganized.
2. leaves dirty dishes in the kitchen sink.
3. ______________________________
4. ______________________________
5. ______________________________
6. ______________________________
7. ______________________________

2. Write on the lines below what characteristics and habits you would like a roommate to have. Remember to write your affirmative statements in the simple present tense.

I want a roomate who . . .

1. cooks often ('cause I can't cook).
2. is tidy ('cause I like a clean apartment).
3. __________
4. __________
5. __________
6. __________
7. __________

'Cause is the reduced form of *because.* It is often used in informal speech.

3. The class will be divided into two groups of students: Group A and Group B. Students in Group A are searching for a roommate and will remain seated. Students in Group B are looking for a place to live. Students in Group B will move around the classroom and introduce themselves to students in Group A. Students in Group A will interview students in Group B about their habits. Students in Group B should repeat the exercise with several students in Group A. When you hear a word you don't know during this activity, ask: "What does . . . mean?"

Write the words you learn from your classmates on the lines below.

__________	__________
__________	__________
__________	__________

Remember to . . .

- speak, respond, and react.
- use sentence parts.
- use rising intonation for *yes/no* questions.
- try to use correct sentence stress and put emphasis on the important words (content words). Make these words longer and higher in pitch.

ACTIVITY **B** 1. Work in groups of three. Each student will need a different coin to use as a marker. Place the coins on **START**. Decide who goes first, second, and third. Student 1 will roll a die and move the number of spaces indicated.

2. When you land on a space, Student 1 reads the question. Student 2 should answer the question and Student 3 should react to the answer. If the third student doesn't react, he or she must go back one space. Students should contine to respond and react to the conversation. Continue the activity until one student reaches the finish line.

START →	What do you usually eat for breakfast?	Do you have any bad habits?	What do you like to do on Saturdays?	What time do you go to sleep during the week?	Does the student to your right eat breakfast every day?
Do you like the city you live in?	Does the person to your right have any bad habits?	How often do you spend time with your friends?	Does the student to your right exercise regularly?	Don't you play any sports? ←	What good habits do you have?
Don't you like to watch sports? →	Do you like to go to movies?	Does the student to your right like outdoor activities?	Does the student to your left eat junk food regularly?	How many hours a week do you study?	**FINISH**

EVALUATION

ACTIVITY **A** Now that you have completed the activities in this chapter, complete the self-evaluation checklist below. Discuss your checklist with a classmate.

Self-Evaluation Checklist

- ☐ I used the simple present tense correctly.
- ☐ I asked and answered negative questions in the simple present tense.
- ☐ I used speaking strategies to help me organize my thoughts during a conversation.
- ☐ I remembered to speak, respond, and react in my conversations.
- ☐ I used sentence parts to react during converations
- ☐ I stressed content words when speaking.
- ☐ I used rising intonation for *yes/no* questions.

ACTIVITY **B** Look back at the chapter and the self-evaluation checklist above. What can you do this week to improve the skills you have learned in this chapter? Talk with a partner and write an action plan for how you can improve your skills this week.

Example *I never use negative questions. I need to work on that. I also need to react to what other people are saying. This strategy will help me expand my conversations. Every time I speak English, I'm going to focus on these two things. I'm going to invite two classmates to chat for 15 minutes before class so we can practice.*

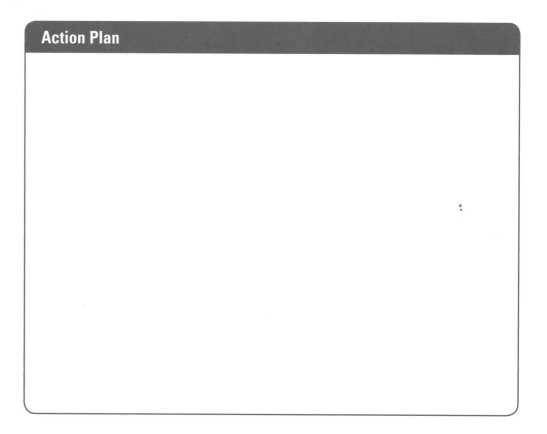

Action Plan

CHAPTER

4 | Can I Make a Suggestion?

GET STARTED

ACTIVITY A
CD 2 Track 1

Listen to the conversations. Write each conversation number below the corresponding picture.

a. ____________

c. ____________

b. ____________

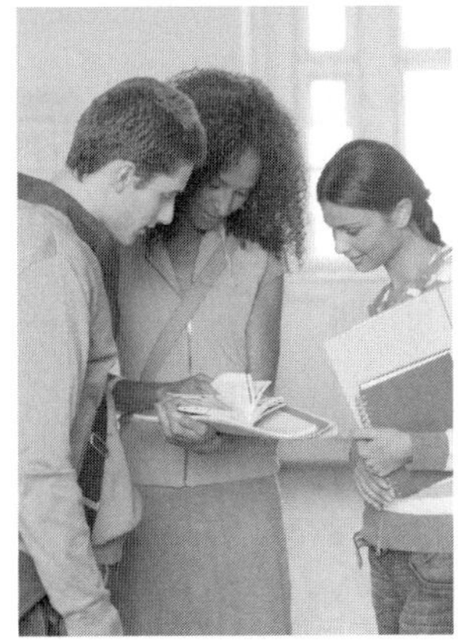

d. ____________

ACTIVITY B
CD 2 Track 2

Listen to the four conversations again. Listen for the bad habit mentioned in each conversation. Write the number of the conversation next to the corresponding bad habit.

____________ He does his homework between classes.

____________ She studies only on the weekends.

____________ He doesn't write down the homework assignments.

____________ He is disorganized.

ACTIVITY **C** **1.** Think of your own study habits. Write down your study habits on the lines below.

My Study Habits
Example: *I study for two hours each day.*
____
____
____
____
____
____

2. What habits do you think help or do not help you learn?

Habits That Help	Habits That Do Not Help
I do homework every day.	*I only study on the weekends.*
______________	______________
______________	______________
______________	______________
______________	______________

ACTIVITY **D**
CD 2 Track 3

1. Listen to two students talk about their study habits.

2. Work in pairs. Use the questions below to talk about your study habits. Ask for repetition when you don't understand something. Don't worry about speaking in complete sentences. React to comments and answers. Refer to the Useful Expressions on the next page as you talk with your partner.

a. How often do you study?

b. What do you do to learn new grammar structures?

c. How often do you listen to the TV news?

d. Why do you have to improve your writing?

e. What do you do to improve your reading comprehension?

f. What do you do to learn new vocabulary words?

Useful
Expressions

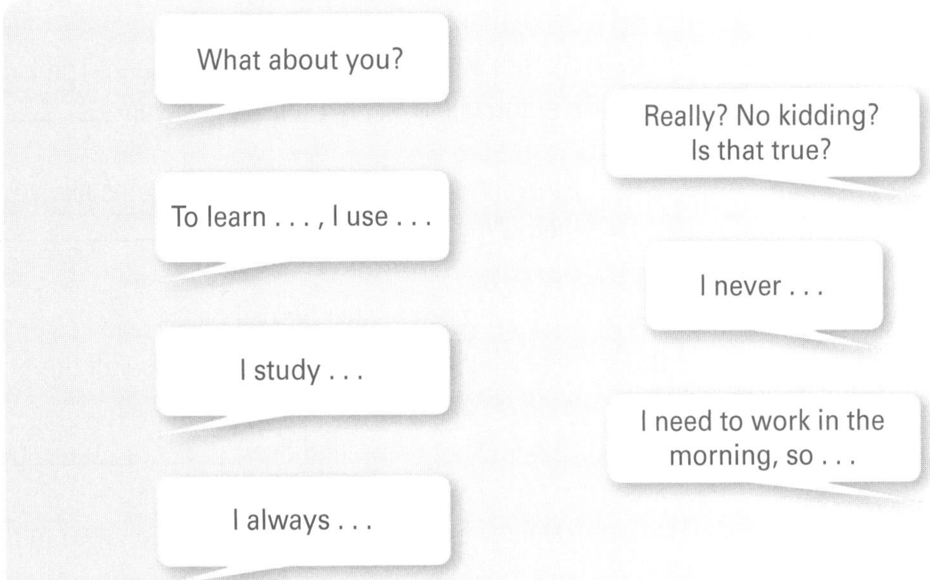

What about you?
Really? No kidding? Is that true?
To learn . . . , I use . . .
I never . . .
I study . . .
I need to work in the morning, so . . .
I always . . .

LEARN AND PRACTICE

SPEAKING STRATEGIES

Hedging

Sometimes when we speak, we do not want to be exact. Hedges are words and expressions that will allow you to be less exact in a conversation. For example, instead of saying, "I'm going to be there *at* five o'clock," you can say, "I'll be there *around* five o'clock." The word *around* suggests that you may not get there exactly at five o'clock. Also, hedges can help you answer difficult questions more politely. Read the examples below.

Hedging with *things/ stuff like that* and *-ish:*

A: I chat with people in English. I use e-mail and chat rooms and { **things like that.** / **stuff like that.** }

B: Oh, really? { **Stuff like that** is not really useful for me. / **Things like that** are not really useful for me. }

Hedging with *-ish* is often used to indicate an approximate time. For example:
I start studying about fiv**ish**. (I start studying around 5:00, but not exactly at 5:00.)

ACTIVITY **A** Read the conversations below. Complete the sentences with *stuff like that, things like that*, or *-ish*. More than one answer is possible.

Conversation 1: Pete is talking to his boss on Monday morning.

Boss: Hello, Pete. How was your weekend?

Pete: Good, thanks. Yours?

Boss: OK. My whole family has colds, though. The kids were sick so they went to bed every night around seven ________ (a).

Everybody's sick . . . You know, it seems like you're so healthy all the time. Why don't you get colds and ________ (b).

Pete: Oh, I don't know. Just lucky, I guess.

Boss: Huh. Maybe it's because you exercise all the time. You're training for a marathon now, right?

Pete: Uh-huh. I get up around five ________ (c) every morning and run 10 miles. Every weekend I work out with weights, bands, and ________ (d).

Boss: Wow! Makes me tired just to think of it!

Conversation 2: Two friends, Yasmin and Julie, make plans for tonight.

Yasmin: What time are we going to the movie theater tonight?

Julie: Oh . . . that's right . . . movie theater. How about seven ________ (e)?

Yasmin: OK. That means the movie ends around nine ________ (f).

Julie: Uh-huh. Can we get some popcorn, chocolate, and ________ (g)?

Yasmin: You bet! ________ (h) is important for having a good time at the movies!

SPEAKING STRATEGIES

Hedging with *About* or *Around*

We can use *about* or *around* to show approximate time and quantity.

For example:

I start studying **about** five. (before or after 5:00)

I start studying **around** five. (a bit before or after 5:00)

I have **about** 100 stamps in my stamp collection. (close to 100 stamps, maybe more or less)

ACTIVITY **B** Complete the conversation below with *around*, *about*, or *-ish*. More than one answer is possible.

Mike, Cindy, and Ryan are talking about a party.

Mike: So, you two need to come over ________ (a) four ________ (b) to help me get ready.

Cindy: Do you have enough places to sit? I think ________ (c) ten people will come.

Ryan: You're kidding? I think it'll be ________ (d) fifteen. What time does the game start?

Cindy: Doesn't it start ________ (e) six thirty?

ACTIVITY **C** Complete the conversations below using the following hedges: *stuff like that, things like that, about, -ish,* and *around.*

Conversation 1

A: Hi, Guys.

B: Hi. You look tired.

C: Hello . . . Yeah, anything wrong?

A: Well, I . . . study, but my grades are not good.

C: Do you study every day though?

B: Uh-huh.

A: I need to study a little every day?

B: Yeah.

C: Also, you might want to study with someone . . .

A: Yeah, that sounds . . .

B: Maybe you could ask other people, like a classmate to help you or ________ (b).

A: Yeah?

A: I'm busy during the day because I work, do laundry and ________ (a), so I, uh, . . . I study on the weekends.

B: Well, that may be your problem.

A: Really?

B: Yeah, ________ (c) helps.

C: Try to do your homework on time, too.

B: Yeah. Oops, my class is about to start. I've got to go. See you guys later.

A: Bye!

C: See ya.

See ya is the reduced form of the phrase *See you later.*

Conversation 2

A: Hi, there.

B: Hi. How're you doing?

C: Hi.

A: Good. Good. Listen, I . . . I have a composition to write, but I, uh . . .

B: Need help?

A: Yeah.

C: What's it about?

B: What's the topic?

A: I need help organizing a paragraph. I need a topic sentence, body, and conclusion.

C: Uh-huh.

B: I can help you tomorrow. Let me see . . . ____________ (d) three.

A: Really? Great! Thanks a million! My class ends at ____________ (e) two ____________ (f), so that's perfect.

B: Just a second. Isn't that assignment due tomorrow at five?

A: Yeah, but I . . . can't do homework at home. Too much noise.

C: Can't you go to a library?

A: I guess I could, but . . .

C: When do you do your homework, then?

A: Between classes.

B: That's not good. You need more time to study.

A: I know, but, uh, . . . can you help me tomorrow?

B: OK! I'll see you tomorrow, then.

A: All right. See ya later.

SPEAKING STRATEGIES

Hedging with *Kind of* or *Sort of*

Kind of (kinda) and *sort of (sorta)* are hedges that are used to say things less strongly. These words are usually used in front of an adjective, verb, or noun. They are informal substitutes for *a little*.

For example:

It's **kinda** difficult (adjective) to study reading.

The instructions in the manual **kind of** tell (verb) us what to do.

It's **sorta** like a chair (noun).

ACTIVITY **D** Read the conversation below. Where can you add *sorta* or *kinda*?

Tricky means difficult or not simple. When something is tricky, you need to pay extra attention to answer correctly.

Amy: What did you think about the test?
John: It was OK. Tricky, though.
Amy: I liked it. I thought it was interesting.
Cathy: I thought it was difficult.
Amy: Well, I tried to answer the questions anyway.
John: Me, too, but sometimes I was not so sure what to answer.
Cathy: I know. Some tests can be tricky.
Amy: Yeah. You're right about that!

SPEAKING STRATEGIES

Hedging with *Like*

The word *like* is also used as a hedge. It often means "not exactly." You may hear it a lot in informal conversation. The word *like* can also be used to exaggerate. Do not use *like* in more formal conversations or situations.

For example:

Hedging with *Like*	Sentence Meaning
He has, **like**, six hours until his flight.	He has to wait for **about** six hours. (not exactly six)
It's, **like**, green-colored.	It's green**ish**, but not exactly green.
That man was so old, I mean, he was, **like**, 100 years old.	He's extremely old, but not exactly 100 years old.
That car she has costs, **like**, a million dollars!	It costs a lot of money, but not a million dollars.

ACTIVITY **E** Follow the directions under each line to complete the conversation. More than one answer is possible in some cases.

A: Hi, there.
B: Hi. When did you get here?
A: ____.
(a) Use two hedges in your answer.

What're is a very informal reduction of *what are.*

B: Really? And . . . what're you doing?

A: ____.
(b) Ask for repetition.

B: What are you doing?

A: ____.
(c) Include *stuff like that* in your answer.

B: Cool. What time are you leaving today?

A: ____. Why?
(d) Use at least one hedge in your answer.

B: I need a ride home today.

A: ____.
(e) React.

B: Where's your car?

A: ____.
(f) Answer with a sentence part.

B: All right, then. See you later.

A: See ya.

ACTIVITY **F**

1. Work with a partner and practice using the hedges from the chapter in a conversation. First, imagine the situation. Use the questions below to help you come up with a scenario.

- Where are you? (Are you in the school cafeteria, in front of a classroom, waiting for the instructor, or someplace else?)
- Who are you? (Are you a student? Is your classmate your friend?)
- What are you doing? (Are you going to a class, relaxing between classes, or are you doing something else?)

2. Write a brief conversation and practice it with your partner. Use at least three different hedges in your conversation.

3. Perform your conversation for the class. Speak clearly, face the audience at all times, and look up when you talk. Do not read the script word-for-word. Instead, try to recreate the conversation without your notes.

Remember to....

- get someone's attention politely.
- react to what the other person says.
- use sentence parts.
- ask for repetition when necessary.

4. As your classmates perform, listen and answer the questions in the chart below.

Questions	Answers
How did the first speaker get the second speaker's attention? (Hi, there. / Hi, Guys. / Hello. / What's up?)	
How did the speakers react to each other? (Really? / Oh. / Yeah. / That's great! / You're kidding?)	
What hedges did the speakers use? (kinda / about / -ish)	

GRAMMAR

Giving Suggestions

When people have problems, we can give them suggestions for solving problems by talking about possible solutions. We can also suggest solutions that indicate a strong necessity or urgency.

We can express possible solutions if we:

- Use the modal *can*. → You **can** try to talk to your instructor about that.
- Use the modal *could*. → You **could** contact your advisor.
- Use *may want to* or *might want to*. → You **might want to** double-check the information.
- Use the modal *would*. → I **would** talk to her.

We can express strong necessity if we:

- Use the modal *should*. → You really **should** take a break now.
- Use *need to*, *have to*, or *have got to*. → You really **need to** see a doctor.
  You **have to** study for this test.
  You**'ve got to** talk to her.

(continued)

GRAMMAR (*continued*)

Look at the examples below.

Problem: I am having problems with my grades.

Possible Solutions:

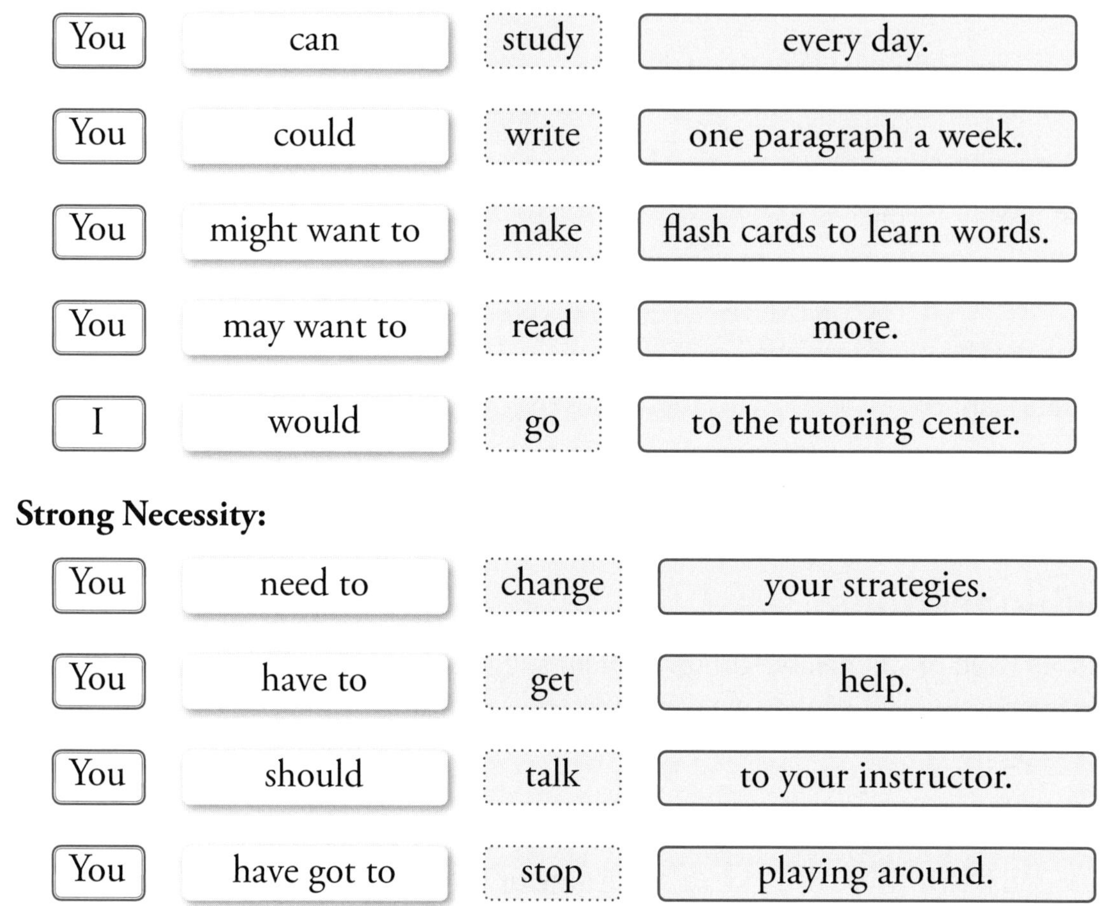

You	can	study	every day.
You	could	write	one paragraph a week.
You	might want to	make	flash cards to learn words.
You	may want to	read	more.
I	would	go	to the tutoring center.

Strong Necessity:

You	need to	change	your strategies.
You	have to	get	help.
You	should	talk	to your instructor.
You	have got to	stop	playing around.

Cultural Note

When you are making a suggestion to someone you don't know very well, it's best to avoid using *need to* or other expressions that indicate strong necessity. Using modals of strong necessity could be misinterpreted as impolite. If you are making a suggestion to someone you don't know very well, use the expressions to suggest possible solutions to problems instead of strong necessity.

ACTIVITY **G** Work in pairs. Match each problem with the corresponding suggestion. Refer to the Useful Expressions below as you discuss your ideas.

Problems	Suggestions
1. I work full-time and go to school. I don't have too much time to study.	**a.** I would find a new home for him. But that's me.
2. My car is a little old and giving me problems. I don't have money for another car.	**b.** I think you really should talk to your roommate about the problem before it ruins your friendship.
3. My roommate is very loud. I like him a lot, but he annoys me sometimes because of the noise.	**c.** You may want to ask your instructor if you can take it early.
4. I want to visit my family in Hawaii. I need to leave on the 5th, but I have a test on the 6th.	**d.** You could try to study on the weekends.
5. I have a dog and I need to move, but I can't find an apartment that allows pets.	**e.** You've got to change seats so that you sit from away from her. You can't let it affect you like that.
6. I have a classmate who always talks to me about silly things during class. She really disturbs me. I think it has started to affect my grades.	**f.** You may want to try to find another car that costs the same price as your own but works better.

Useful
Expressions

I think number . . . goes with letter . . .
This is just a guess, but I think number 2 goes with this one.
Yeah. That's what I think.
I have no clue.

ACTIVITY H Listen to the conversations. Write down the suggestions that you hear in each conversation.

CD 2 Track 4

Conversation 1: ______________________________

____

Conversation 2: ______________________________

____

Conversation 3: ______________________________

____

Conversation 4: ______________________________

ACTIVITY I

1. Work with a partner. Read each problem and then write two or three suggestions about how to solve the problems. You can suggest possible solutions or you can express strong necessity.

I'm afraid of speaking English outside of class.	I study every weekend, but I can't get good grades.
______________	______________
______________	______________
______________	______________

I'm afraid of making mistakes when I speak.	I have a hard time using different verb tenses.
______________	______________
______________	______________
______________	______________

2. Discuss your suggestions with the class. Your classmates should continue the conversation by reacting to your suggestions.

REVIEW: LISTENING STRATEGIES AND PRONUNCIATION

Sentence Stress

To use correct sentence stress, emphasize the most important words with a higher pitch and a longer stressed syllable. That is, make the vowel sound longer. If you emphasize words by making them longer and higher, people can understand the main meaning of what you are saying more easily.

(continued)

As you learned in Chapter 3, we emphasize important words in English. How are individual words emphasized to make **sentence** stress?

CD 2 Track 5

Listen to the following sentence and the emphasis on the content words.

You are all wonderful English students, and I like teaching you very much.

Words that are not content words are not stressed. We usually do not stress these types of words:

Pronouns: *he, she, it, them, they*

Articles: *a, an, the*

Prepositions: *for, to, over, under, from*

Auxiliary Verbs: *can (go), could (have), is (going)*

CD 2 Track 6

A successful English student is talking to her friend. Listen and repeat the conversation making sure you use proper sentence stress. Underline the stressed words in each sentence.

A: You know, um . . . I really don't know how to do well in English class.
B: Really? Uh, what do you have a problem with?
A: Well, um . . . I don't do well on tests and things like that . . .
B: Uh-huh.
A: And, I don't remember too much vocabulary.
B: Oh, I know what you mean.
A: Really?
B: Yup. Maybe you need to study a different way.
A: What do you mean?
B: Well, um . . . if you . . . you only look at the book to study . . .
A: Uh-huh.
B: You don't really learn words.
A: Really?
B: Uh-huh. You might want to make flash cards and carry them with you.
A: Oh.
B: You can study them while you are waiting in line, riding on the bus, or stuff like that.
A: I see.

SPEAKING STRATEGIES

Speaking Politely: Conversations Have a Beginning, a Middle, and an End

Polite conversations generally have a sequence that includes a beginning, a middle, and an end. Look at the parts of this conversation about a problem.

Beginning: Opening Greeting

A: Hi, there.
B: Hey.

Beginning: Noticing Something is Wrong

A: You look worried. What's the matter?

Middle: Explaining Your Problem

B: Well, I . . . um . . . I'm having problems at work . . .
A: Oh, I'm sorry to hear that.
B: It's the new manager. She is really mean to me!
A: That's terrible.
B: Yeah.

Middle: Offering a Suggestion

A: You might want to talk to Human Resources about it.
B: Yeah. I have to be brave.
A: You could set an appointment . . .
B: Uh-huh.
A: And you really need to describe her behavior.
B: Uh-huh.
A: Without calling names or judging. Just describe what she does.

Middle: Accepting the Suggestion

B: That's a great idea.

OR

Middle: Rejecting the Suggestion, Explaining Why It Will Not Work

B: I don't think I can do that! I'm too shy.

End: Final Comments / Closing Greeting / Say Good-bye

A: I hope things get better.
B: Thanks.

ACTIVITY **K** Refer to the parts of a conversation in the box on page 62. Then read the conversations. What is the purpose of each part of the conversations? Choose a purpose from the box and write it next to the corresponding conversation part.

greeting	accepting/rejecting the suggestion
offering a suggestion	noticing something is wrong
explaining a problem	

Conversation 1:

A: How are you guys doing?
B: Jennifer! What's up?
C: What's up, Jen?

_______________ (a)

B: Hey, you don't look so good.
C: Yeah. You look beat, what's . . . why are you so tired?

_______________ (b)

A: Well . . . alright, alright. I just . . . I've been studying and my grades still aren't very good.
C: Well, how often are you studying?
A: Well, you know, I work during the week . . .
B: Uh-huh.
A: And then I have other things to do, um . . . like my laundry.

_______________ (c)

C: Yeah.
A: And, you know, stuff like that, so, you know, I really only get to study on the weekends.
B: Um, maybe that's part of the problem.

_______________ (d)

A: Yeah, I guess, um . . . I guess I should study a little bit more every day.
C: That might help.

_______________ (e)

Conversation 2:

A: What's wrong? } ______ (a)

B: I'm a little worried about the test on Monday.
A: You haven't studied?
B: I have, but, uh . . . I am still sorta confused . . . about two things . . . minor things, you know? } ______ (b)

A: Why don't you clarify those with your instructor tomorrow? } ______ (c)

B: We don't meet on Fridays. } ______ (d)

A: Oh, can you send her an e-mail? } ______ (e)

B: She doesn't really like us to e-mail her with questions. } ______ (f)

A: Um . . . maybe you could call her during her office hours. } ______ (g)

B: That's a good idea. } ______ (h)

A: She will certainly help you. It's her office hours after all!
B: You're right. I'll do that.

REVIEW AND EXPAND

CD 2 Track 7

1. Listen to a group of students playing a problem/solution game.
2. Work in groups of four. Student 1 should choose one of the problem cards from page 175 and explain the problem to the group.
3. Students 2, 3, and 4 should use the cards on page 176 and write possible solutions to the problem. Students 2, 3, and 4 should each give a suggestion to solve the problem. Student 1 will respond to each suggestion and decide which suggestion best solves the problem.
4. Student 2 then picks a problem card and repeats the exercise. Continue the exercise until all four students have chosen a problem. Refer to the Useful Expressions on the next page to help you in your discussion.

Useful
Expressions

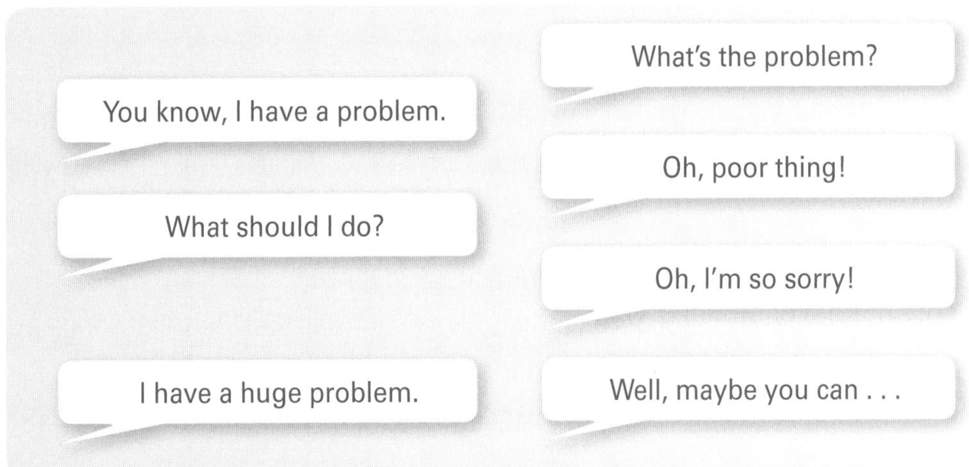

What's the problem?
You know, I have a problem.
Oh, poor thing!
What should I do?
Oh, I'm so sorry!
I have a huge problem.
Well, maybe you can . . .

ACTIVITY **B** Work in groups of three. Choose one of the three scenarios below. Read each situation and follow the directions.

Scenario 1:

You are roommates. You are at home and you are having a conversation about these problems:

a. One of you likes to stay up late and watch TV, but the others don't like it. You can hear the TV from all the bedrooms.

b. One of you never remembers to pay the bills on time!

c. One of you is always talking on the phone!

Discuss your habits and give suggestions on how to solve the problems.

Scenario 2:

You all work together in the same office. You have a conversation about these problems:

a. One of you takes two-hour lunch breaks. (Lunch breaks are supposed to be only one hour.)

b. One of you always leaves the office kitchen messy after using it.

c. One of you always talks to the others when they are trying to work.

Discuss your problems and give suggestions on how to solve the problems.

Scenario 3:

You are classmates in a very difficult writing class.

a. One of you has a very difficult essay to write.

b. One of you needs help with grammar.

c. One of you needs help with organizing your writing.

Talk about the problems you are having and give suggestions to each other.

EVALUATION

ACTIVITY **A** Now that you have completed the activities in this chapter, complete the self-evaluation checklist below. Discuss your checklist with a classmate.

Self-Evaluation Checklist

- ☐ I used a variety of hedges while speaking.
- ☐ I gave possible suggestions as well as suggestions expressing strong necessity.
- ☐ I correctly used modals to give suggestions and to offer solutions to problems.
- ☐ I stressed the most important words in a sentence.
- ☐ I made certain that my conversations contained a beginning, a middle, and an end.

ACTIVITY **B** Look back at the chapter and the self-evaluation checklist above. What can you do this week to improve the skills you have learned in this chapter? Talk with a partner and write an action plan for how you can improve your skills this week.

Example **I've noticed that I always use *have to* or *need to* when I want to give a suggestion. I need to use other words to differentiate the possible suggestions from the ones expressing strong necessity. Every time I talk, I'm going to focus on using *can, could,* or *might want to* when I make suggestions.**

Action Plan

CHAPTER

5 | Is That Really Necessary?

GET STARTED

ACTIVITY A
CD 2 Track 8

Listen to a college student explain all of her responsibilities for the week. Put a check mark ✓ next to each task that she needs to do.

☐ organize her room	☐ study for a test
☐ clean her closet	☐ prepare a speech
☐ schedule her activities	☐ do homework
☐ call a friend	☐ prepare dinner

ACTIVITY B
CD 2 Track 9

1. Listen to two students comparing their answers to Activity A.
2. Work with a partner and discuss your answers to Activity A. Remember that when you talk, you can ask for repetition, use sentence parts, and employ other speaking strategies. If you do not know how to say something, ask your instructor, "How do you say . . . ?" Refer to the Useful Expressions on the next page to help your discussion.

Useful
Expressions

She said . . .

She also needs to . . .

She has . . .

Uh-huh. She has to . . .

I believe she has to . . .

ACTIVITY **C** Look at the verbs below. Write collocations for the verb in each box.

Do	Take	Organize	Schedule
do homework	take a test	organize your time	schedule your classes

Hang Up	Put Away	Fix	Straighten
hang up your jacket	put away your CDs	fix the car	straighten the bedroom

ACTIVITY **D** Match each sentence with the correct collocation from the box.

1. You do this after you wake up in the morning. ______
2. You do this after you come back from school. ______
3. You do this after a baseball comes through your window. ______
4. You do this when you have been studying and need a rest. ______
5. You do this when you move into a new apartment. ______
6. You do this when you have papers covering your desk. ______
7. You do this after you get off the couch. ______
8. You do this when you come inside after shoveling snow. ______

a. hang up your coat
b. put away your books
c. make the bed
d. straighten pillows
e. take a break
f. fix the window
g. straighten your desk
h. put away your belongings

CD 2 Track 10

1. Look at the picture of Ellen's room. Listen to two people talking about Ellen's messy room.
2. Work with a partner. Discuss the problems that you see in the room and what Ellen needs to do to fix them. Try to use as many collocations as you can in your discussion. Refer to the Useful Expressions on the next page to help your conversation.

Useful
Expressions

Yep is an informal way of saying *yes.* *Nope* is an informal way to say *no.* Some people also say *nah* for *no* and *yeah* for *yes* in informal situations.

Uh-huh. /Yep. / Nope.

I know.

I think she also needs to . . .

She's gotta . . .

I don't think that is really important.

Yeah. Right!

LEARN AND PRACTICE

GRAMMAR

Explaining Necessity and Obligation

We often have to talk about necessities (things we need to do) and obligations (things we have to do). For example, you may need to discuss your grade on a test with your instructor (necessity) or pay your bills (obligation). Let's learn the most frequent ways to talk about necessities and obligations in conversational English.

Look at these examples:

I	have to	pay	the phone bill.
I	should	talk	to my instructor today.
I	need to	decide	on what class I want to take.
I	have got to	buy	a dictionary.
I'm	supposed to	talk	to the counselor.

Many English learners think that *must* is frequently used to express necessity. In actuality, *must* is rarely used in conversational English.

(continued)

GRAMMAR (*continued*)

Using the Expressions

Have to (hafta), *have got to* (have gotta), and *need to* (needta) indicate a sense of urgency.

For example:

- I **have to** get out of here.
- **I've got to** finish my presentation.
- Today I **need to** clean my room. It's a real mess!

Should and *be supposed to* are often used for less urgent needs or things that can be negotiated. When expressing necessity or obligation, *should* is more often used with the subject *I* (rather than *you*).

- I **should** take a break on Sunday. I'm really stressed.
- I'**m supposed to have** lunch with a friend on Friday, but I **have to** do my English homework. I guess I can call my friend to see if we can have lunch next week instead.

ACTIVITY A **1.** Think about your obligations. Write the things you have to do today, tomorrow, and this weekend in the chart below. Do not use complete sentences.

Today	Tomorrow	This Weekend
study for a test	call my brother	do homework
a. ______	c. ______	e. ______
b. ______	d. ______	f. ______

2. Now, write complete sentences about your obligations on the lines below. Make sure you use *have to, have got to*, and *need to* for the more urgent needs, and *should* and *be supposed to* for the things you can negotiate.

a. ______

b. ______

c. ______

d. ______

e. ______

f. ______

CD 2 Track 11

1. Listen to a pair of students talking about their obligations for the week.
2. Work with a partner. Discuss the obligations that you wrote in Activity A. Remember to respond and react to your partner.

GRAMMAR

Asking for Help

In Chapter 2, we learned that we can use modals to ask for personal information. We can also use modals to ask for help. When we have too many things to do, or we need to do something we are not good at, we may need to ask for help.

Modals—verbs can be used to politely ask for help in both private and public situations. A private situation is when there are only a few speakers and they know each other well. A public situation is when there are a number of speakers that do not know each other very well, or do not know each other at all.

- *Can* is less formal and is frequently used when the speakers have a close relationship. It's usually used in private situations, such as in conversations between two siblings, a husband and wife, and close friends.

  Can | you | help | me with my homework?

- *Could* is more formal and is often used when the speakers are not very familiar with one another. Could can be used in both private and public situations, such as in conversations between a student and instructor, a boss and employee, and a salesperson and a customer.

  A: Excuse me?

  B: Yes?

  A: Could | I | try | this skirt on?

- *Would* is often used in public situations when a request is made, such as in a classroom or in a meeting.

  Would | you | explain | that again, please?

The word *please* is usually used at the end of a polite request for help.

ACTIVITY **C** Read each scenario below. Would the speakers use *can, could*, or *would* to ask for help? Circle the correct answer. Before you choose your answer, determine how well the speakers know each other and whether they are in a private or public setting. More than one answer may be possible.

a. A brother and a sister are at home. The sister asks her brother if she can borrow his mp3 player. **can** **could** **would**

b. Two coworkers, who are also very good friends, are talking. One coworker asks the other coworker to use her pen. **can** **could** **would**

c. The instructor is teaching a class with 25 students. One of the students interrupts the class to ask the instructor to clarify a point. **can** **could** **would**

d. Five students are working in a group. One student interrupts a group member to ask him to speak more slowly. **can** **could** **would**

ACTIVITY **D** Work with a partner. Read the information in the first column. With your partner, write a necessity or obligation that the speakers could be discussing. Then write a request for help that one of the speakers could make.

Speakers/ Situation	Necessity or Obligation	Request for Help
close classmates / private situation	*I've got to turn in my homework for tomorrow, but I don't understand the assignment.*	*Can you help me, please?*
mother and daughter / private situation		
boss and employee / public situation, such as a meeting with other employees		
coworkers who do not know each other well / public situation		

Remember, after a modal, you have to use the base form of a verb. It is incorrect to use the infinitive: *to* + verb.

GRAMMAR

Responding to Requests for Help

When someone asks us for help, we need to respond appropriately. We may be able to help the person, we may be unsure if we can help the person, or we may not be able to help at all. Look at the examples of ways we can respond.

Yes Responses	*Maybe* Responses	*No* Responses
• Sure, it's no problem. • I'd be glad to. • Yes, I can.	• I'm not sure. Let me think about it. • Maybe, but I don't know for sure. • Possibly. Let me get back to you.	• I'm sorry, but I can't. • I'm afraid I can't help you. • I wish I could, but I can't.

If you ask for help and receive a *no* response, it is polite to say, "Thanks anyway." Remember, saying "thanks anyway" should only be used when you receive a *no* response. Don't say it when you hear a *yes* respsonse.

ACTIVITY **E**
CD 2 Track 12

Listen to the phone calls that Christina makes. How do Christina's friends respond to her requests? Write the responses you hear on the lines below.

Conversation 1. All right. I'll take you.

Conversation 2. ______________________________

Conversation 3. ______________________________

Conversation 4. ______________________________

Conversation 5. ______________________________

SPEAKING STRATEGIES

Speaking Politely: Conversations with a Beginning, a Middle, and an End

Polite conversations generally have a sequence that includes a beginning, a middle, and an end. The middle portion of each conversation can vary depending on what the speaker is saying. For example, if the speaker is asking for help, the middle portion of the conversation will include a request for help and a response. Read the example below.

Beginning: Opening Greeting

(Telephone rings.)

A: Hello?
B: Mona?
A: Hey, Jake. What's up?

Middle: Indicating there is a problem

B: I need your help.
A: Uh-huh.

Middle: Explaining the problem

B: I need to read a book for my literature class . . .
A: Uh-huh.
B: And I know you have it.
A: Which one?
B: It's a classic—*Of Mice and Men.*
A: Oh, yeah, I do have it.

Middle: Making a request

B: Can I borrow it for a couple of weeks?

Middle: Responding to a request

A: Oh, sure. I'm not using it.

Middle: Asking a question

B: Great! When is a good time to pick it up?
A: After lunch today.
B: I'll be there.

End: Reacting to the response

B: Thanks a lot!
A: No problem.

ACTIVITY **F** Read the conversations below and put the correct number next to the corresponding part of each conversation. You may not need to use all of the parts in each conversation.

Parts of the Conversation:

1. Opening greeting
2. Indicating there is a problem
3. Explaining the problem
4. Making a request
5. Responding to a request
6. Asking questions
7. Thanking and reacting to the response

Conversation 1:

Christina: Excuse me, um, Luke?
Luke: Uh-huh? } ____________

Christina: You know what?
Luke: What? } ____________

Christina: I have a movie to return to the library . . .
Luke: Uh-huh. } ____________

Christina: So . . . since you work next to the library . . .
Luke: Uh-huh? } ____________

Christina: Could you stop by . . . and return this movie for me? } ____________

Luke: Oh, I should return my books, too. They are way overdue! } ____________

No problem. I'd be glad to.

Conversation 2:

Christina: Hello, Marco. I'm glad I saw you.
Marco: Hey! } ____________

Christina: Can you help? This box . . . ugh . . . is too heavy. Can you carry it for me? } ____________

Marco: Oh, I'm soooo sorry, but I can't help you. I gotta catch the bus and I, um . . . uh-oh, I see it at the stop right now! } ____________

Christina: Oh, well.
Marco: Sorry! Gotta go!
Christina: That's OK. } ____________

Conversation 3:

Christina: Missy!

Missy: Oh, hi, Christina. What's up? } ____________

Christina: You know I'm supposed to give a presentation in my history class next week, right? } ____________

Missy: Uh-huh.

Christina: I was wondering . . .

Missy: Yeah? } ____________

Christina: Could you . . . um . . . videotape it for me?

Missy: Next Wednesday? } ____________

Christina: Yeah, next Wednesday at five.

Missy: Well, um . . . possibly. Let me get, uh . . . let me get back to you on that. I'll tell you on Friday. } ____________

Christina: Oh, OK. Thanks. } ____________

Missy: Hey, I've gotta get going. I'm late for class.

Christina: OK, thanks.

ACTIVITY **G**

1. The class will form two lines and will stand facing one another. Students across from each other should pretend that they are good friends, family, or close classmates.
2. Students in Line 1 should explain a necessity or obligation to the student across from them and then make a request for help. Students in Line 2 should respond to the request. Be sure that all conversations have a beginning, a middle, and an end. Then students in Line 1 move down one space and begin the activity again with a new partner. (The person at the end of Line 1 will go to the beginning of the line.)

PRONUNCIATION

Reductions (Reduced Forms)

CD 2 Track 13

When people talk, they sometimes push words together and change the way they pronounce them. This is called a reduction or a reduced form. Many of the modals we use to ask for help can be reduced.

Listen to the examples below:

- would you = *wooja*
- could you = *cooja*
- can you = *canya*

(continued)

PRONUNCIATION (*continued*)

Many of the verbs used to express necessity can also be reduced. Listen to these examples:

- have to = *hafta*
- need to = *needta*
- have got to /'ve got to = *('ve) gotta*
- supposed to = *suppozta*

ACTIVITY H CD 2 Track 14

Lee is in the international student office filling out a form. Many offices at universities are informal places. Lee asks someone for help. Listen for the reductions and fill in the lines with the words you hear.

A: ____________ (a) please help me, um, with this form?
B: You ____________ (b) sign your name here.
A: Oh, OK. ____________ (c) tell me, uh, what to put in this blank?
B: Hmm, you ____________ (d) put if you're married there.
A: Thanks. ____________ (e) also tell me what to put here?
B: Sure. Let's see, you ____________ (f) put where you're from there.
A: Thanks for all your help.
B: You're very welcome.

ACTIVITY I CD 2 Track 15

Listen to the conversation again. Listen to the reductions in the sentences below and repeat them after the speaker.

would you: *Wooja* please help me, um, with this form?
have to: You *hafta* sign your name here.
can you: Oh, OK. *Canya* tell me, uh, what to put in this blank?
have got to: Hmm, you'*ve gotta* put if you're married there.
could you: Thanks. *Cooja* also tell me what to put here?
need to: Sure. Let's see, you *needta* put where you're from there.

Cultural Note It's very important to remember that reductions are not mistakes. Instead, they are simply a natural part of the spoken language. Speakers use reductions in both formal and informal situations. However, they are more common and acceptable in informal situations. In formal situations, people often speak more carefully, especially if they are talking with their boss, talking in front of a class, or when they are on a job interview. In these situations, using too many reductions could be considered inappropriate English.

ACTIVITY J
CD 2 Track 16

Listen to the speakers say the reduced and nonreduced forms of modal phrases. Repeat the sentences after the speakers. Listen again and write whether you hear the reduced or nonreduced form in the sentence.

a. Would you please help me, um, fill out this form? ____________
b. Would you please help me, um, fill out this form? ____________
c. You have to put your signature here. ____________
d. You have to put your signature here. ____________
e. Oh, all right. Can you tell me, uh, what goes in this blank? ____________
f. Oh, all right. Can you tell me, uh, what goes in this blank? ____________
g. Let's see . . . you've got to put down if you are married there. ____________
h. Let's see . . . you've got to put down if you are married there. ____________
i. Could you tell me where I put my social security number? ____________
j. Could you tell me where I put my social security number? ____________
k. You have to write it right here. ____________
l. You have to write it right here. ____________

ACTIVITY K
CD 2 Track 17

Listen to the conversations and circle if you hear the nonreduced or reduced form of each modal phrase.

Conversation 1:	would you	wooja
Conversation 2:	could you	cooja
Conversation 3:	kind of	kinda
Conversation 4:	can you	canya
Conversation 5:	have got to	've gotta

SPEAKING STRATEGIES

Hesitation Strategies

CD 2 Track 18

In casual conversation, people use hesitation strategies. A hesitation strategy is a sound, word, or expression used to get extra time to think while you are speaking. These sounds and expressions are very common in informal speech, and they can make you sound more fluent because they help you speak without too many unexpected silences. In formal speech, people try not to use too many hesitation strategies.

Here are some hesitation strategies that can be used for informal conversation:

- uh
- um
- hmm
- let's see
- (draw out the word: *Sooo . . .*)
- well
- and
- (pause)
- let me think

ACTIVITY L CD 2 Track 19

Listen to each conversation. Write down the hesitation strategies you hear. Some conversations may have more than one. Listen again and check your answers.

1. ______________________
2. ______________________
3. ______________________
4. ______________________
5. ______________________
6. ______________________

ACTIVITY M

1. Your instructor will ask you the questions below. Answer each question and practice using hesitation strategies when you speak.
    - What's your favorite kind of music?
    - What do you like most about your hometown?
    - Who is your favorite celebrity and why?
    - Where are you going to spend your next vacation?

2. Work in groups of three or four. Each group member should take turns asking one of the questions below. The other members of your group should answer each question and use hesitation strategies to gain time to think.
    - What's your favorite type of food?
    - What's your favorite movie of all time?
    - Who is someone you admire? Why do you admire this person?
    - Where is your favorite place to relax?

- Who is your best friend? Why?
- What's your favorite sport?
- Who's your favorite athlete?
- How often do you go to a movie theater?
- Your own question: ____________________

GRAMMAR

Making Appointments

We can also use what we've learned about explaining necessity and obligation to learn how to make appointments.

ACTIVITY **N**
CD 2 Track 20

Listen to people making appointments. Each person is expressing a problem as he or she asks for an appointment. Write down the problem you hear in each conversation.

Conversation 1. ____________________

Conversation 2. ____________________

Conversation 3. ____________________

Conversation 4. ____________________

Conversation 5. ____________________

Conversation 6. ____________________

ACTIVITY **O**
CD 2 Track 21

Listen to the appointments again. In some conversations you will hear modals. If you hear questions with modals, write them down. If you don't hear any questions with modals, write *no modals*.

Conversation 1. ____________________

Conversation 2. ____________________

Conversation 3. ____________________

Conversation 4. ____________________

Conversation 5. ____________________

Conversation 6. ____________________

SPEAKING STRATEGIES

Speaking Politely: Conversations with a Beginning, a Middle, and an End

As we discussed earlier in the chapter, polite conversations generally have a sequence that includes a beginning, a middle, and an end. Just as interactions for requesting help follow a structure, interactions where people make appointments follow a structure, too. Look at the structure for making appointments below.

Beginning

1. Identify yourself.
2. Explain your problem.

Middle

3. Ask and answer questions about your problem.
4. Negotiate a time and day for your appointment.
5. Ask for and answer personal information politely.

End

6. Confirm the time and day of your appointment.
7. Thank the person and say good-bye.

ACTIVITY **P** Look at the parts of the conversation in the box above. Read the conversations below and write the number that corresponds to each part of the conversation on the line beside it.

Conversation 1: (Telephone rings.)

A: Good morning. Dr. Wilson's office.
B: Hello, this is Janet Peterson. My son is a patient of Dr. Wilson's. } ______

A: Uh-huh?
B: I'm calling to make an appointment for him. He has a bad cough. } ______

A: All right. Let me see . . . is Friday morning at ten OK?
B: Um, let me check . . . Friday morning. . . . Sure. That's fine. } ______

A: All right, then. You have an appointment with Dr. Wilson on Friday at ten. } ______

B: Thank you very much.

A: You're welcome. Bye-bye.
B: Bye. } ______

Conversation 2: (Telephone rings.)

A: Good morning, Community College Health Center, may I help you? ________

B: Yes, hi. This is Matt Santana. I'm a student.

A: Uh-huh?

B: I'm calling because, uh, I need to see a doctor. ________

A: Uh-huh.

B: I . . . um, . . . have a bad cold and a stuffed-up nose.

A: Yes, I can hear that. OK, then, can you come in this afternoon at two?

B: Uh, I, um, . . . um, I'm supposed to give a presentation today at that time. ________

A: OK. How about, um, ...after the presentation?

B: Yes. I can talk to my instructor. It should be OK.

A: All right. Can I have your name again?

B: It's Matthew Santana.

A: Can you spell your last name? ________

B: S-A-N-T-A-N-A.

A: And may I have your student ID number?

B: 441-62-7873.

A: OK, then. You have an appointment at the health center this afternoon around 3:30 . . . ________

B: Thanks a lot.

A: And you need to bring your student ID when you come. ________

B: No problem. See you at 3:30.

A: Thanks.

ACTIVITY **Q**

1. Half of the class will be Group A. The other half of the class will be Group B. Students in Group A need to make an appointment over the telephone. Students in Group A should write below what office they are calling and what their problem is.

   Office: ________________________________

   Necessity: ________________________________

2. Students in Group B are the receptionists who schedule the appointments. A student in Group A will call a student in Group B and explain his or her problem. Be sure that your conversation includes a beginning, a middle, and an end.

3. Several groups will perform their conversation for the class. The class should make sure that each conversation includes a beginning, a middle, and an end. The class should also discuss the appropriateness and politeness of the speakers.

LISTENING STRATEGIES

Listening for the Main Ideas

When you listen for the main ideas, your goal is to remember what happened in general rather than to remember details. One strategy you can use is to make mental pictures. As you listen, try to imagine a picture of what is happening in your mind. This will help you both understand and remember the information better.

ACTIVITY R
CD 2 Track 22

Close your books and listen to the conversation. As you listen, imagine the events in the story as Claire tells it. After you listen, open your book and answer the question.

What happened to Claire? Write down what happened first, second, third, and so on in your own words.

____

____

____

____

____

____

____

ACTIVITY S

1. Work with a partner. You and your partner will discuss three topics. As your partner talks, imagine a picture in your mind of what he or she is telling you. Do not take notes.

   Tell your partner about:

   - the things you have to do to stay healthy (sleep, eat, exercise, drink a lot of water, etc.).
   - the things you have to do this week (take a test, make an appointment, buy groceries, etc.).
   - the things you want to do to have more fun (go to the movies, have dinner with friends, go hiking, etc.).

2. After you have finished, your instructor will assign you a new partner. You need to tell your new partner the information about your old partner. Can you remember it all?

REVIEW AND EXPAND

ACTIVITY **A**

1. Work in groups of four. Each student will write down a necessity or obligation and a request for help on a card. For example:

> **Necessity:** *I have to study for my math test.*
>
> **Request for help:** *Can I borrow your math notebook?*

2. Place all of the cards in a pile. Student 1 picks a card from the pile and reads it silently. Then Student 1 puts the card down and explains his or her necessity or obligation and asks for help.
3. The other three group members will respond to the request. Student 2 should say *no* politely and give an excuse. Student 3 should answer *maybe* and give an explanation. Student 4 should answer *yes* and conclude the conversation. Repeat the activity until all group members have asked for help.

Remember to . . .

- react.
- ask for repetition if you don't understand something.
- ask your instructor if you don't know how to say something.
- hesitate.
- use sentence parts.

ACTIVITY **B**

1. Work in pairs. One student is an assistant who will schedule the appointment. The other student is calling to make an appointment.
2. Choose one of the scenarios below and call to make the appointment. Make sure you negotiate a time and day that works for you.

Location	Reason for Calling
doctor's office	You have back pain.
school counselor's office	You need help with your academic plan.
lawyer's office	You need to draft a will.
supervisor's office	You need to talk about a personal issue at work.

3. When you are ready, perform your conversation in front of the class. Your classmates have to guess where you are and who you are. They will also point out any language that is inappropriate for the situation.

EVALUTION

ACTIVITY **A** Now that you have completed the activities in this chapter, complete the self-evaluation checklist below. Discuss your checklist with a classmate.

Self-Evaluation Checklist

- ☐ I used various expressions to explain a necessity or obligation.
- ☐ I used modals to ask for help.
- ☐ I made sure that my interactions had a beginning, a middle, and an end.
- ☐ I used hesitation strategies properly.
- ☐ I listened for main ideas by building mental pictures.
- ☐ I was able to use reductions (reduced forms) correctly.

ACTIVITY **B** Look back at the chapter and the self-evaluation checklist above. What can you do this week to improve the skills you have learned in this chapter? Talk with a partner and write an action plan for how you can improve your skills this week.

Example *When I'm talking to someone, I always expect to hear each syllable clearly. I need to focus on learning reductions. I'm going to do a search on the Internet for common reductions and learn them. I'll try to use them as I talk and use that knowledge when I'm listening. I hope it will help me understand what I hear better.*

Action Plan

CHAPTER

6 | Could I Borrow This?

GET STARTED

ACTIVITY A CD 2 Track 23

1. Listen to the conversations. What problems do the students have? Write the problems on the lines.

a. His class notes are bad. He doesn't have time to take a note-taking class.

b. ______________________________

c. ______________________________

d. ______________________________

2. Work with a partner. Match the beginning of each sentence to a problem. In some places, more than one answer is possible.

Sentence Beginnings	Problems
1. I don't understand ___	a. sick.
2. I can't ___	b. the simple present.
3. The book is ___	c. a meeting.
4. I don't know ___	d. the homework that is due tomorrow.
5. I am ___	e. come tomorrow.
6. I have a hard time ___	f. understanding the class.
7. I have ___	g. too difficult.

ACTIVITY B **1.** Write three problems you sometimes have. Use the beginning of the sentences from Activity A to help you.

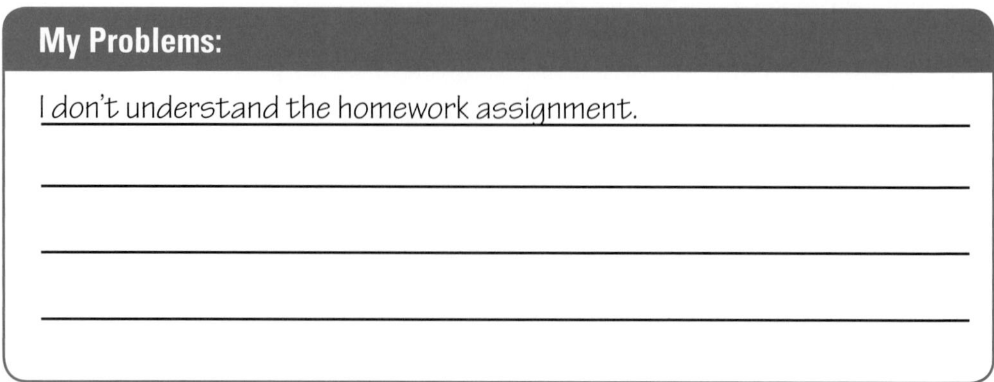

CD 2 Track 24

2. Listen to a student discuss her problem with a classmate.

3. Work with a partner and talk about your problems. Find out if your partner has the same problems. Refer to the Useful Expressions below to help you.

Useful ***Expressions***

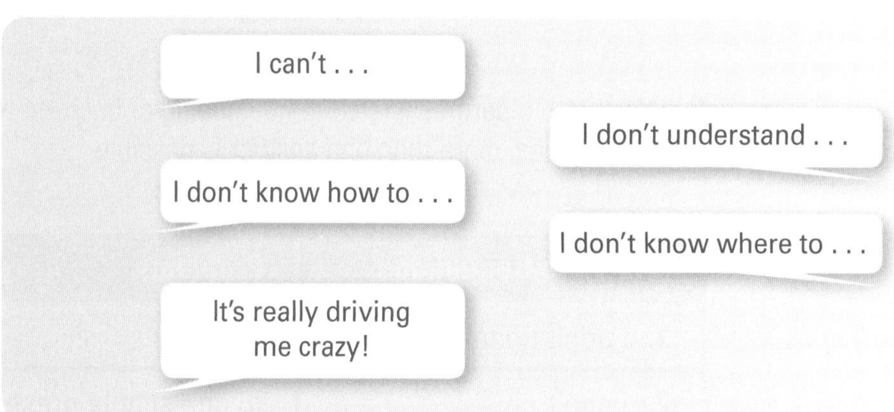

I can't . . .
I don't understand . . .
I don't know how to . . .
I don't know where to . . .
It's really driving me crazy!

Remember to . . .

- react. (Are you kidding? / Really? / Oh. / Yeah. / Good. / I see.)
- hesitate. (Um . . . / Uh, well . . . / Let's see . . . / Let me think . . .)
- ask for repetition. (Sorry? / Excuse me? / Pardon me? / What was that?)
- use hedges. (things like that / kinda / about / around)
- emphasize the important words with intonation (make the important words longer and higher in pitch).

LEARN AND PRACTICE

LISTENING STRATEGIES

Answering Questions When Listening for Main Ideas

In Chapter 5, you were introduced to the concept of listening for the main idea. The main idea is general information that you don't need to write down to remember, such as how many people are involved in a conversation, where it takes place, and what happens in general. In order to answer questions related to the main idea correctly, it's important to understand how to do so.

Follow these steps:

- Read the questions you have to answer BEFORE listening.
- Do not read or write while listening. Listen ONLY.
- IMAGINE the situation as if it were a movie. Visualize the scene as you listen to the conversation.
- ANSWER the questions after you have listened to the conversation.

ACTIVITY A Listen to the conversations between students and instructors. Listen for the main idea and number the pictures from 1 to 4 in the order you hear them.

CD 2 Track 25

a. ____________________

c. ____________________

b. ____________________

d. ____________________

ACTIVITY B
CD 2 Track 26

Close your book. Then listen to the first conversation again. Imagine what is going on. Use the space below to draw a simple picture of what is happening.

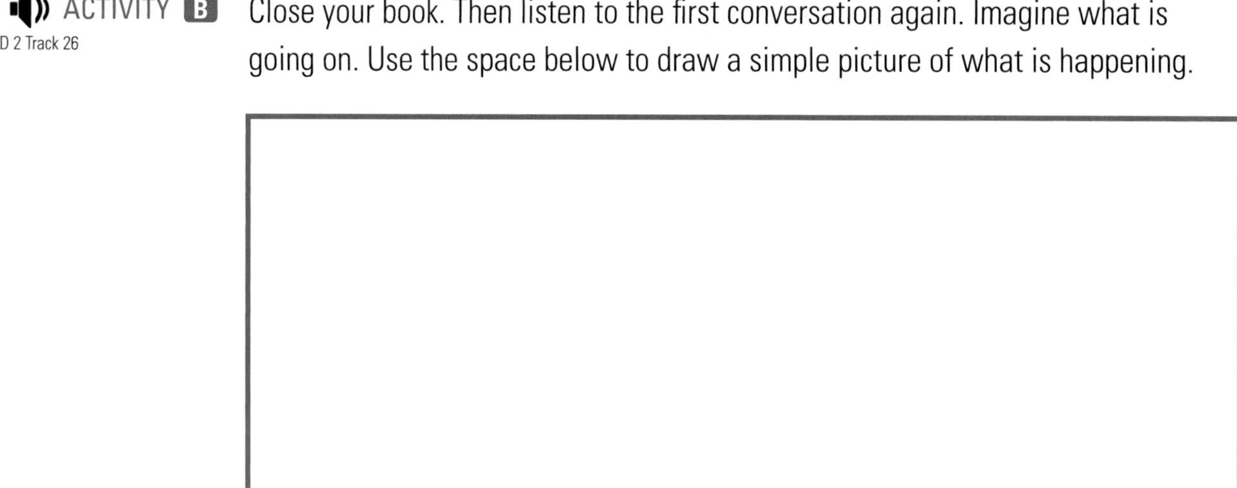

ACTIVITY C
CD 2 Track 27

Read the questions below before you listen to the conversation. Close your book and listen to the conversation. Then open your book and circle the correct answers.

1. What is the student's problem?
   - a. He is very busy.
   - b. He doesn't understand the homework.
   - c. He can't come to tomorrow's class.
   - d. He didn't do well on the test.
2. What is the student requesting?
   - a. He's asking if he can miss tomorrow's class.
   - b. He's asking if he can carry the instructor's CD player.
   - c. He's asking if he can talk with the instructor.
   - d. He's asking if he can retake the test.

ACTIVITY D
CD 2 Track 28

First, read the two questions. Then close your book. Listen to the conversation and make a mental picture of what is happening. Do not take notes. Then open your book and circle the correct answer to each question.

1. What is the student's problem?
   - a. She has a doctor's appointment next week.
   - b. She needs to leave town for several days.
   - c. She's got to help her family move.
   - d. She has to study for another test.
2. What is the instructor's reaction?
   - a. He gives the student permission, but tells her that she can't have any more absences.
   - b. He explains the rules and doesn't give the student permission.
   - c. He is very rude and doesn't give the student permission.
   - d. He says that he can't help because of the college rules for absences.

REVIEW: PRONUNCIATION

Reductions (Reduced Forms)

CD 2 Track 29

When talking about problems, we frequently use *have to* and *have got to.* These forms are often reduced and sound like ***hafta*** and ***gotta.***

Listen and repeat the informal and formal pronunciation.

a. You *hafta* be careful so you don't get ripped off.	**(Reduced)**
b. You *have to* be careful so you don't get ripped off.	**(Nonreduced)**
c. I've *gotta* bend over backwards to make him happy.	**(Reduced)**
d. *I've got to* bend over backwards to make him happy.	**(Nonreduced)**
e. I *hafta* help because she has her hands full with the kids.	**(Reduced)**
f. I *have to* help because she has her hands full with the kids.	**(Nonreduced)**
g. You*'ve gotta* live and learn.	**(Reduced)**
h. You*'ve got to* live and learn.	**(Nonreduced)**

ACTIVITY **E** Work with a partner. Practice saying each sentence from the box above out loud. Your partner will monitor your use of reduced and nonreduced words. Then switch roles and listen as your partner reads each sentence.

Cultural Note

During conversations, speakers sometimes use idioms. Idioms are expressions that have one meaning when the words are put together and a different meaning when the words are used separately. Idioms are used frequently in conversation, and understanding them can improve your ability to understand others.

Here are a few common English idioms and their meanings:

to get ripped off: to be cheated, to pay too much for something, or to buy something that is not of good quality

to bend over backwards: to try very hard to please someone

to have one's hands full: to be very busy with many different things and not be able to do anything else

GRAMMAR

Making Polite Requests (Asking for Permission)

In Chapter 5, you learned how to ask others for help with a specific task. Sometimes, we need to ask others if we have permission to do something. This is called asking for permission or making a polite request. When we have problems we need help with, we often make requests. Look at the examples below.

Problem: My cell phone is dead.

Request: Can I use your cell phone?

Problem: I don't have my book with me today.

Request: Could I borrow your book?

Problem: I didn't take the test last class

Request: May I talk to you about it?

May is not commonly used to ask for help, but it is commonly used to ask for permission. In fact, *may* is as common as *could* and *can* when asking for permission.

Could I or *could you* sound more formal and polite than *can I* or *can you.* You might want to choose *can* for more informal situations or when you are not requesting something very important. *May* is the most formal and polite of the modals used to ask for permission.

Cultural Note It's important to make sure that you are being polite when making a request. Research shows that native English speakers consider politeness mistakes more serious than grammatical mistakes. Therefore, grammar and politeness come hand-in-hand when learning a language.

ACTIVITY **F** Read the problems below. Write a polite request next to each of them. Be sure to use *can, could,* or *may* in your request for permission.

Problem 1. Oh, no. I can't find my pen. ______________________

Problem 2. My phone battery died. ______________________

Problem 3. This is really heavy. ______________________

Problem 4. I didn't come last class. ______________________

ACTIVITY **G**

1. Work with a partner. Each pair should have a sheet of paper. Your instructor will assign you one of the sets of roles below. One of you will write down a problem and then make a polite request for permission. The other person will write a response to the request. Then you will post your request and response on the wall of the classroom.

Roles	
Student—Instructor	Pharmacist—Customer
Friend—Friend	Bookstore Clerk—Customer
Neighbor—Neighbor	Student—Counselor

2. With your partner, walk around the room and read each request. Check if they are polite and grammatically correct. Mark any corrections on the paper.

GRAMMAR

Making Promises

Often when we make a polite request or ask for permission, we also make a promise in order to persuade the other person to say yes.

For example:

- Can I borrow ten bucks? I'll pay you back tomorrow.
- May I borrow your notes? I'll return them at the end of class.
- Dad, could I use your car tomorrow? I'll fill up the gas tank for you.

So, when we make promises, we often use *will* or *won't.*

I	will	wash	it for you.
I	won't	lose	it.

ACTIVITY H Write down a promise that Speaker A could make in each conversation below. Try to use *will* or *won't* in your promise.

Example

A: Mom?

B: Yes?

A: Can I use your cell phone this afternoon?
I won't use it unless it's an emergency.

B: Sure. No problem. Just be careful not to lose it.

Conversation 1:

A: Bro?

B: Huh?

A: Can I use your new tennis shoes? ____________________

B: OK. Take them!

Conversation 2:

A: Do you have your wallet?

B: Yes.

A: Can I borrow ten bucks? ____________________

B: Sure.

Conversation 3:

A: Can I borrow your laptop tomorrow?

B: What for?

A: My computer is not working well, and I need to do my homework.
____

B: OK.

ACTIVITY I Imagine you need something from a classmate you know well. Write down what you need, your polite request for permission, and your promise. Use *I need to, I have to, I've got to, I should,* or *I'm supposed to.*

Example I'm supposed to meet with Professor Calandra in five minutes, but I forgot to bring my book. Can I borrow yours? I'll be back in 20 minutes tops.

a. Item Needed: ____________________
Request: ____________________
Promise: ____________________

b. Item Needed: ___________________________

Request: ___________________________

Promise: ___________________________

c. Item Needed: ___________________________

Request: ___________________________

Promise: ___________________________

d. Item Needed: ___________________________

Request: ___________________________

Promise: ___________________________

SPEAKING STRATEGIES

Ways of Saying *Thank You* and *You're Welcome*

It is considered polite to say *thank you* and *you're welcome* in most conversations, whether they are formal or informal situations. In English, there are many ways of saying *thank you* and *you're welcome*. Look at the examples below.

THANK YOU:

Thank you so much.
'Preciate it. (informal)
Thanks. (informal)
Thank you. I appreciate it. (formal)
Thank you very much. (can be formal)

YOU'RE WELCOME:

a smile or nod (informal)
Uh-huh. (informal)
No problem. (informal)
You're (very) welcome. (formal)
Sure. (informal)

ACTIVITY **J** In pairs, go around the classroom borrowing objects from your classmates. Be sure to make a polite request for permission. Use the various expressions above to say *thank you* and *you're welcome*. Refer to the Useful Expressions below to help you.

Useful ***Expressions***

Can I borrow your . . . ?

May I use your . . . ?

SPEAKING STRATEGIES

Starting and Ending Polite Requests

When we have a conversation where we make polite requests, we usually follow these steps:

1. **Greet** the other person. (We greet or get the attention of the person and say we need to talk with him or her.)
2. **Explain** the problem.
3. Make a polite **request.** (Tell the person what we would like.)
4. **Negotiate** a solution. (The person may talk about what to do or just tell you *no*.)
5. Say **thank you.** (Say *thank you* even if the person says *no*.)

ACTIVITY **K** Read the conversation. Look at the five steps for starting and ending polite requests. Decide which lines of the conversation correspond to each step. Write the numbers on the lines.

Greet ________ **Explain** ________ **Request** ________
Negotiate ________ **Thank** ________

(1) A: May I speak with you, Mrs. Chen?
(2) B: Sure.
(3) A: I have jury duty tomorrow.
(4) B: OK.
(5) A: Uh-huh. So, I can't come to class.
(6) B: Yeah, I guess not.
(7) A: So, um . . . can I turn in my homework assignment on . . . Friday instead?
(8) B: Oh, um . . . Could you send it to me by e-mail?
(9) A: Actually I, um, . . . I don't have an e-mail account.
(10) B: Oh, you don't?
(11) A: Nope.
(12) B: Well, then, um, go ahead and hand it in on Friday. I can't allow that to happen often though.
(13) A: I understand. I'm sorry. Thanks. I appreciate it.

ACTIVITY **L** The conversation below is not in order. Read each section of the conversation on pages 97 and 98. Choose the correct conversation part from the box and write it on the line.

Greet the other person.	Explain the problem.	Say *thank you.*
Make a polite request.	Negotiate a solution.	

Conversation	Answer
Gabriella: I, um, . . . I have a problem. **Dr. Garcia:** OK . . . **Gabriella:** Well, I, um, . . . I've gotta travel to Brazil next week. My dad is really sick. **Dr. Garcia:** Oh, I'm sorry to hear that.	a. ______________________
Gabriella: May I come in, Dr. Garcia? **Dr. Garcia:** Sure. Come on in. **Gabriella:** Thanks. **Dr. Garcia:** How can I help you?	b. ______________________
Gabriella: Yes. So, I, um, . . . I was wondering . . . **Dr. Garcia:** Uh-huh? **Gabriella:** May I miss one whole week of class?	c. ______________________
Gabriella: That's what I'll do. Thank you, Dr. Garcia. I appreciate your honesty. **Dr. Garcia:** I wish you the best, Gabriella.	d. ______________________

Dr. Garcia: Actually, Gabriella, I understand your problem... **Gabriella:** Mm-hmmm . . . **Dr. Garcia:** But, uh . . .The writing class is a five-unit class, and your grades are, um, so-so . . . **Gabriella:** Yeah, I know. **Dr. Garcia:** So, I honestly don't think you can afford to miss a whole week. **Gabriella:** Oh, . . . **Dr. Garcia:** I don't think you can miss a whole week and pass. **Gabriella:** OK . . . I see. . . . **Dr. Garcia:** I'm sorry. **Gabriella:** Soooo, do you think I should drop the class then? **Dr. Garcia:** I believe that is the best thing for you to do. **Gabriella:** Uh-huh. **Dr. Garcia:** Then . . . next semester, you can try it again. **Gabriella:** Uh-huh. **Dr. Garcia:** How about that? **Gabriella:** Uh . . . I think you're right. **Dr. Garcia:** Yeah.	**e.** ______________________________

ACTIVITY **M**

1. Work with a partner. Your instructor will post blank sheets of paper on the walls around the classroom. Each pair will stand in front of a sheet of paper.
2. You instructor will make a polite request from the box below. You and your partner have to write an explanation of the problem that the instructor could have. You will have two minutes to write.

Example **Request:** Can I borrow your history book?

Problem: I left my history book on the bus this morning, and I have an open-book test this afternoon.

Requests
Can I use your cell phone for just a minute?
Could I borrow your notebook?
May I use your calculator?
Can I ask you a few questions about the last class?

3. After the two minutes are up, walk around the classroom and read the other explanations. Correct any mistakes in grammar that you notice. As a class, vote for the funniest and the most unusual explanations.

ACTIVITY **N** Work with a partner. Choose the type of relationship that you have, such as brother/sister, instructor/student, or boss/employee. Create a dialog where you greet one another, explain a problem, make a polite request, negotiate a solution, and say *thank you.* Write your dialog on a sheet of paper. After you create the dialog, stand up and perform it in front of the class. You can glance at the script as you speak, but you cannot read the script.

SPEAKING STRATEGIES

Making a Polite Request on the Telephone

It is also important to speak politely when leaving a voice message for someone who is not available to speak. When leaving a message over the telephone, an interaction usually has four parts:

1. Identify yourself by saying, "This is . . ."
2. Explain the problem and express a necessity.
3. Make a polite request.
4. Leave your contact information and say thank you.

(continued)

SPEAKING STRATEGIES (*Continued*)

Example:

> Hello, Dr. Will. This is Peter Chang, from your English 101 class. . . I'm calling 'cause I'm supposed to take a make-up test with you tomorrow, but I, uh . . . I'm sorry to tell you that I . . . I am very sick . . . with the flu, and I . . . can't leave home for a couple of days. Um . . . could I take the test some other time? I'd appreciate it if you could call me back at 345-6789. Thanks.

ACTIVITY **O** Read the voice messages below. Write a polite request that you think each person might make.

Voice Message 1:

Hi, Lea. It's me. I'm calling you because, um . . . I'm going to the zoo with Charles tomorrow, and I . . . um . . . my camera is broken . . .so I was wondering ______________________________ tomorrow? I'll give it back to you the day after tomorrow. Give me a call and let me know. Thanks.

Voice Message 2:

Hi, Darlene, this is John from work. I need to do some work in the office tomorrow, and it would be great if I could use that software program you showed me yesterday. So, um ______________________________ I'll give it back to you on Monday. If that isn't possible, that's OK. Thank you very much.

Voice Message 3:

This message is for Jessica Montalvao. Hi, Jessica, this is your ESL instructor. It's time for our monthly meeting. ______________________________
I'm in the office every day from 9:00 until noon. Talk to you soon. Good-bye.

ACTIVITY **P** Listen to two voice messages. On the lines below, write down who is calling, what the problem is, and the request that you hear.

CD 2 Track 30

Voice Message 1:

Who: ______________________________

Problem: ______________________________

Request: ______________________________

Voice Message 2:

Who: ______________________________

Problem: ______________________________

Request: ______________________________

SPEAKING STRATEGIES

Clarity and Politeness in Voice Messages

Sometimes voice messages don't have all of the four parts needed to make them clear and polite. Look at the examples below.

Example 1: Hi, it's your student George. I'm just calling to let you know that I can't go to class today. Thank you.

This message is unclear because a instructor can have several classes and more than one student named George.

Example 2: Hi. This is Ruanda. I can't bring the homework today, so, um . . . I'll bring it tomorrow. Bye.

This message is somewhat impolite. The student is not making a polite request here. Instead, the student is telling the instructor what she is going to do. It is always important to use modals to make a polite request, or a message can sound impolite.

ACTIVITY Q Read each of the messages below. Check ✓ if the message is unclear, impolite, or both. Discuss your answers with the class.

Message	Unclear	Impolite	Both
Hi, Dr. Chavez, it's me. I won't be able to go to the student-instructor conference today at 3:00 because of some personal problems I have to take care of. I'll talk to you in class today and explain everything. Bye.			
Hi, Dr. Wen. I can't come to class today. Bye.			
Hello, Dr. Chen. This is Carina Soto. I'm calling because I'm not going to be able to go to school tomorrow because I have jury duty. So, um . . . I won't be able to take the test. I'm guessing it's OK for me to take the test some other time, right? All right, then. I'll see you next week. Bye.			
Hello. This is your student from English 104 calling. I have to leave early today. I hope that's OK. Bye.			

ACTIVITY R Listen to the following voice messages and check ✓ unclear, impolite, or both.
CD 2 Track 31

	Unclear	Impolite	Both
Message 1			
Message 2			
Message 3			

ACTIVITY S 1. It is your turn to leave a message for a instructor. Complete the information.

Your identification: This is ____________ from your ____________
____
Your problem: ________________________________
____
Your request: ________________________________
____
Your contact number: __________________________

2. Work with a partner. One person will read the outgoing message below. Then the other person will leave a message. Use your notes from Part 1 to help you, but do not read them. Hesitate to help you think while you speak. Your partner will listen and monitor your message to be sure that you are clear and polite.

Outgoing Message:

"You have reached the office of Dr. Butler. I'm either away from my desk or with a student. Please leave a short message, and I'll call you back as soon as possible. Thank you."

3. Now switch roles with your partner and repeat the activity.

REVIEW AND EXPAND

CD 2 Track 32

1. Listen to two students simulating a discussion between a professor and a student.
2. Make two lines facing each other. Students in Line 1 are students. Students in Line 2 are professors. Simulate a conversation between a student and a professor. The students should greet the professor, explain the problem, make a request and a promise, and thank the professor. The professors should ask questions and negotiate a solution to the problem. Refer to the Remember to . . . box on the next page to help your discussion.

Remember to . . .

- ask for repetition. (Pardon me? / Excuse me? / Sorry?)
- hesitate. (Well, let me see . . . / Um . . . / Uh . . .)
- use more formal and polite English because you are speaking with professor and you want to make a polite request—you can hedge, hesitate, use reductions, and use sentence parts, but don't overuse these strategies in this formal situation.
- use *I need to, I have to, I've got to, I should,* or *I'm supposed to* when explaining your problem.
- use *may I, can I,* or *could I* when making your request.
- negotiate a solution to the problem with your professor.

ACTIVITY **B**

1. What other times do you need to make a polite request? Think of some more formal situations. Work with a partner and write your answers in the boxes below.

Who	Problem	Request
my boss	I have a doctor's appointment.	May I leave work early today?

2. Now change partners. Tell your partner about one of your problems. Create and practice a conversation.

Remember to . . .

- use new ways of saying *thank you* and *you're welcome* in your conversation.
- start and finish your conversation appropriately.
- negotiate a solution to your problem.
- ask for repetition.

EVALUATION

ACTIVITY **A** Now that you have completed the activities in this chapter, complete the self-evaluation checklist below. Discuss your checklist with a classmate.

Self-Evaluation Checklist

- ☐ I made polite requests and asked for permission.
- ☐ I was able to explain a problem and make a promise.
- ☐ I used *can I, could I,* and *may I* correctly.
- ☐ I properly started and ended requests for permission.
- ☐ I left polite and clear voice messages.
- ☐ I was able to listen for main ideas.
- ☐ I used reductions (reduced forms) properly.

ACTIVITY **B** Look back at the chapter and the self-evaluation checklist above. What can you do this week to improve the skills you have learned in this chapter? Talk with a partner and write an action plan for how you can improve your skills this week.

Example I worry a lot about grammar and sometimes forget about being polite when making a request. I want to practice making polite requests. I'm going to ask a classmate to practice with me. We can choose different situations, review the grammar and the sequence of the conversation, and make sure that we are using polite language. I can do this once or twice a week.

Action Plan

CHAPTER

7 | I Used to do That.

GET STARTED

ACTIVITY A
CD 3 Track 1

Listen to the conversations. Write the conversation number below each picture.

a. ____________________

c. ____________________

b. ____________________

d. ____________________

ACTIVITY B
CD 3 Track 2

Listen to the conversations again. Write down what each person *used to* do and what they do now.

Conversation 1	Conversation 3
Now: ____________________	Now: ____________________
Used to: ____________________	Used to: ____________________
Conversation 2	**Conversation 4**
Now: ____________________	Now: ____________________
Used to: ____________________	Used to: ____________________

ACTIVITY **C** Think about things you used to do in the past that you don't do anymore. Why have things changed? In the chart below, write what you used to do, what you do now, and the reason why you changed your habits.

I used to . . .	Now I . . .	Reason
____________________	____________________	____________________
____________________	____________________	____________________
____________________	____________________	____________________
____________________	____________________	____________________

ACTIVITY **D** Listen to three students discuss their answers to the chart from Activity C. Work in groups of three. Discuss the chart from Activity C with your partners.

CD 3 Track 3

Remember to . . .

- react to what your group members say.
- ask more questions.
- ask for repetition when you don't understand.

LEARN AND PRACTICE

SPEAKING STRATEGIES

Using Encouragers

During conversations, people try to show that they are interested in what the other person is saying. They nod their heads and use sounds or words that show they are paying attention. This speaking strategy is called using encouragers. Look at the examples of some common encouragers:

Uh-huh. Mm-hmm. Right. Yeah.

I see. Oh! Really!

ACTIVITY A Listen to the conversations. Complete the blanks with the encouragers you hear.

CD 3 Track 4

Conversation 1:

A: Hi, there!
B: Hey!
A: You look relaxed!
B: I went to the springs with my family.
A: For the 4th of July?
B: ____________________
(a)
A: What a great way to spend the holiday.
B: ____________________
(b)
A: Do you guys always go there for the 4th?
B: Um . . . well . . . we are doing that now . . .
A: ____________________
(c)
B: . . . but, uh, . . . we didn't use to go anywhere . . . until the beaches here got too crowded . . .
A: ____________________
(d)
B: And . . . you know . . . too many people . . .
A: ____________________
(e)
B: So, um . . . we decided to go somewhere else . . . y' know . . . away from, you know . . .
A: Yep. I hear you.
B: What did you do?
A: Well, I just stayed home . . .
B: Good.
A: . . . avoided the beaches for the same reason.
B: No kidding!

Conversation 2:

A: Hello?
B: What's up?
A: Not much. Cleaning my apartment.
B: Oh, that's exciting.
A: Yeah . . . I, I really, uh . . . it's never, never finished, but maybe some day . . .
B: ____________________
(f)
A: Yeah, I have to do the laundry and straighten up the family room . . .
B: Mm-hmm . . . you know, when I lived in Brazil . . .

A: ________________
(g)

B: I never did anything at home.

A: ________________
(h)

B: I had a maid who did everything.

A: ________________
(i)

B: I wasn't rich or anything . . .

A: Uh-huh.

B: It's just very normal to have live-in maids there.

A: I wish I had a maid!

B: No kidding! I used to spend all my time at home studying. No chores!

A: ________________
(j)

B: Now I spend *hours* doing stuff like cleaning bathrooms and things I hate!

A: I hear ya . . . I don't mind cooking, but cleaning . . . nope!

B: ________________
(k)

A: . . . Don't like it.

B: So, anyway . . . I was wondering . . .

ACTIVITY **B** Read the conversations below. Which text looks more like a real, informal conversation? Work with a partner and discuss your reasons for choosing the text you chose.

Text 1	Text 2
A: How are you? **B:** I'm fine, thanks. And you? **A:** Good, thanks. Do you want to sit down here with me and eat your lunch? **B:** Sure. Thanks. **A:** You're welcome. How was your weekend? **B:** It was really good. I went to Las Vegas with some friends. **A:** You went to Las Vegas? That's exciting! **B:** Yes, it is. But it was an expensive trip. So, I shouldn't spend a lot of money for the rest of the week. *How're* is an informal reduction of *how are.*	**A:** Hi! How're you? **B:** Great. You? **A:** Pretty good. Wanna sit down here with me and eat your lunch? **B:** Um, sure. Thanks. **A:** No problem. Uh, how was your weekend? **B:** Really good. **A:** Mm-hmm? **B:** Went to Las Vegas with some friends. **A:** Wow! You went to Las Vegas. That's kinda exciting. **B:** Yep. But I, uh, well, . . . it was pretty expensive. **A:** I see. **B:** So, I kinda can't spend a lot of money for the rest of the week.

Cultural Note You may be unsure about using encouragers because you think it interrupts the speaker. However, if you do not use encouragers, some people may think that you are not interested in the conversation. Using encouragers is a very important part of English conversation. In fact, encouragers are commonly used in both formal and informal conversations.

ACTIVITY **C** Look back at Text 2 on page 108. Underline the sentence parts, hedges, hesitations, and encouragers that you find. Then compare your answers with the person seated next to you.

ACTIVITY **D**

1. Look at the conversation below. You need to change it into a conversation that seems more like a real, informal conversation. Use at least one encourager, one hesitation, one hedge, and one sentence part in your conversation. Write the new conversation in the box below.

   A: Hello, Tom. How are you?
   B: I'm fine. How about you?
   A: I'm OK. How was your test this morning?
   B: It was bad. It was very difficult. I was confused.
   A: I'm sorry about that.

   ____
   ____
   ____
   ____
   ____
   ____
   ____
   ____
   ____

2. Practice your conversation with a partner. After you practice, your instructor will ask you to perform your conversation for the class. Stand up, look at your partner, and try to recall the conversation without reading your notes. If you forget part of the conversation, use a hesitation strategy, look down at your paper, and then look up again to speak.

Using Adverbs to Identify Tense

When we think about time, we think about the present, the past, and the future. In order to identify if someone is talking about the present, the past, or the future, we need to listen for adverbs of time. We should not listen for verb tense because the same verb tense may be used to express ideas in the present, past, and future.

For example:

1. I have a class at two o'clock <u>every single day</u>.
2. I have a class at 2 o'clock <u>tomorrow</u>.

Sentence 1 describes a habitual action (present), whereas Sentence 2 expresses a future obligation. However, both sentences contain the verb *have* in the simple present.

3. I'm leaving <u>tomorrow</u>.
4. I'm leaving <u>right now</u>.

Sentence 3 describes a future action (tomorrow), whereas Sentence 4 expresses an idea of an action that is happening at the time the person is speaking (present). However, both sentences contain the present progressive form of the verb *leave*. Therefore, we need to learn how to identify when an event is taking place by listening to adverbs of time, rather than verb tense.

In order to identify time, we can think of it as a physical position. For example, what is *behind* us is past, what is *with* us often is present, and what is *ahead of* us is future.

Every day is often with me, so it's present.

Last week is behind me, so it's past.

Tomorrow is ahead of me, so it's future.

(continued)

LISTENING STRATEGIES (*continued*)

Now look at some examples of adverbs of time:

every day	never	last month
in two days	last weekend	tomorrow
always	a minute ago	in a minute
last week	five years from now	this morning
when I was a child	when I turn thirty (I'm 20.)	

ACTIVITY **E** Look at the example of adverbs of time from the box above. Classify the expressions of time above into *past*, *present*, and *future*. Write the words in the correct box below.

Past	Present	Future

ACTIVITY **F** Stand up. Your instructor will say adverbs of time from the list on the next page. You need to decide the time—past, present, or future.

When you hear:

- **Past** . . . you need to take one step backward.
- **Present** . . . you need to raise your hand.
- **Future** . . . you need to take one step forward.

Adverbs of Time	
two weeks ago	a second ago
last year on my birthday	every two days
every birthday	next March
every spring break	every New Year's Eve
last summer	a month ago
next semester when classes start	in a second
the end of every month	every summer

ACTIVITY G
CD 3 Track 5

Listen for the adverbs of time in each conversation. Are the conversations in the past, present, or future? Write the answers on the lines.

Conversation 1: past ____________

Conversation 2: ____________

Conversation 3: ____________

Conversation 4: ____________

GRAMMAR

Talking about Past Events

We can use the simple past tense to talk about events that happened in the past. In the simple past tense, the verb form changes. The symbol [P] represents the past tense. Regular verbs in the simple past tense are formed by adding *-ed* to the end of the verb. Irregular verbs in the simple past tense vary in form. We have to memorize the irregular forms. Look at the examples below.

Regular Past Tense Verbs	Irregular Past Tense Verbs
cooked	got (get)
watched	put (put)
listened	made (make)
called	left (left)

(continued)

To form the simple past tense, the main verb changes to the past tense form.

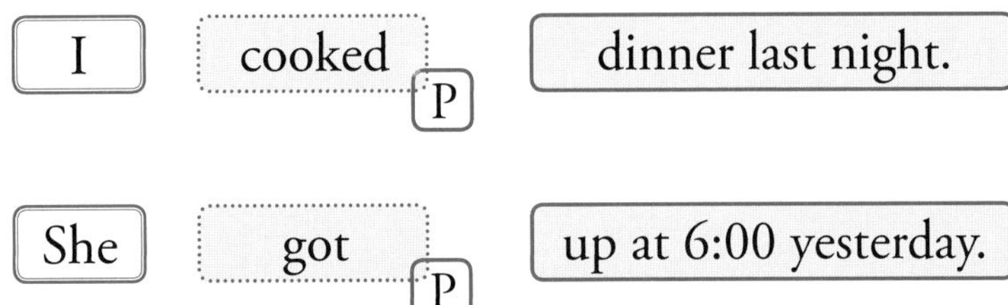
I
cooked
P
dinner last night.
She
got
P
up at 6:00 yesterday.

For *yes/no* questions and negative statements, the auxiliary verb takes the past tense form.

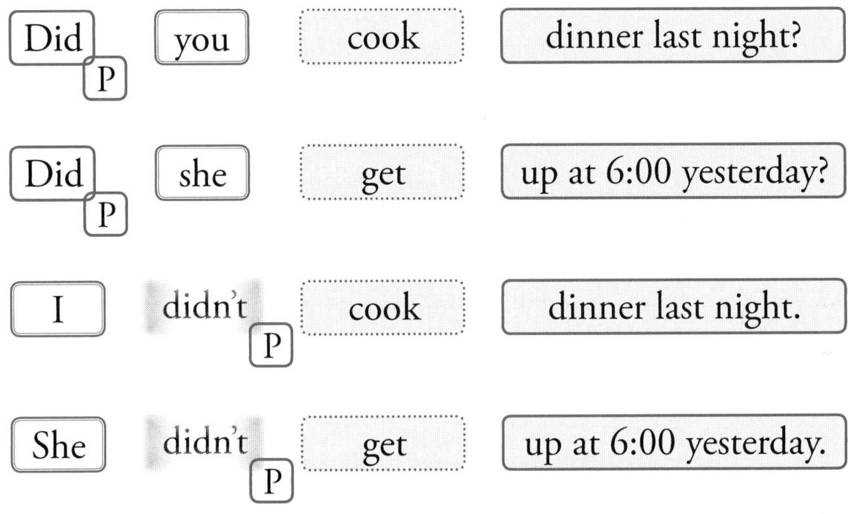
Did
P
you
cook
dinner last night?
Did
P
she
get
up at 6:00 yesterday?
I
didn't
P
cook
dinner last night.
She
didn't
P
get
up at 6:00 yesterday.

ACTIVITY **H**

CD 3 Track 6

1. Listen to a group of students completing an activity about past events.
2. Your class will be divided into two teams. One team is Team X and the other team is Team O. Each team will take turns and choose a square from the board below. Your instructor will give each team a verb and ask the team to come up with a sentence using the verb in the past tense. If possible, each team should use an adverb of time in their sentence.
3. If the sentence is correct, the square is marked with the team's symbol (*X* or *O*). If the sentence is incorrect, the other team can give a sentence and steal the square. The winner is the team that gets three of their symbols in a row. Refer to the Useful Expressions on the next page to help your discussion.

	Left	**Center**	**Right**
Top			
Middle			
Bottom			

Useful
Expressions

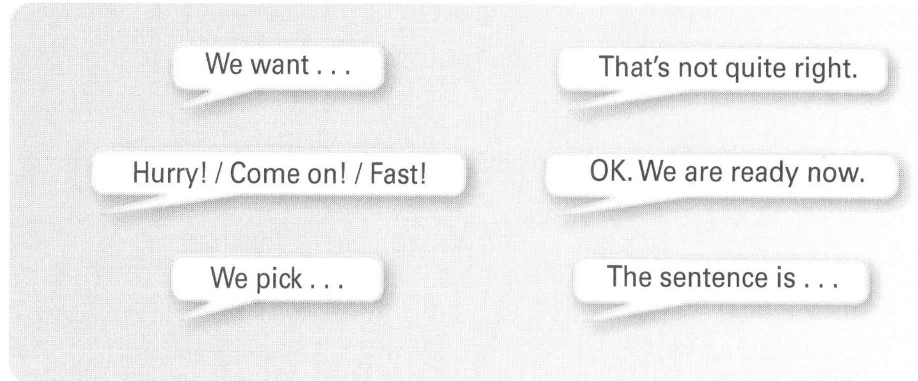

We want . . .
That's not quite right.
Hurry! / Come on! / Fast!
OK. We are ready now.
We pick . . .
The sentence is . . .

CD 3 Track 7

1. Listen to a student giving an excuse as to why she did not bring a CD to class.
2. Work in pairs. One student is Student A. The other student is Student B. Student A asked to borrow Student B's new CD yesterday. Student B forgot to bring it to school. Student B should come up with an excuse about why he or she forgot the CD and explain it to Student A. Student A should listen to the explanation, react, and use encouragers. Use the audio, the verbs in the box below, and the Useful Expressions on the next page to help your conversation. Then switch roles with your partner and complete the activity again.

Regular Past Tense Verbs	Irregular Past Tense Verbs
cooked breakfast	got out of bed (get)
watched the morning news	put on makeup (put)
listened to the radio	made breakfast (make)
called my mother	left the house (leave)
lifted weights	took the bus (take)
waited for the bus	drove my kids to school (drive)
missed the bus	did my English homework (do)

Useful
Expressions

GRAMMAR

Contrasting Past and Present with *Used To*

When we talk about things that were habits in the past, we use *used to*. *Used to* is very common in conversational English. It is used just like a modal verb. Look at the example below.

I | used to | exercise | every day before I had kids.

The sentence above means the person does not do the activity anymore. *Used to* can be used to contrast past events with present events.

Questions and negatives with *used to* are formed with *did* and *didn't*. Look at the examples below.

***Yes/No* Questions:**

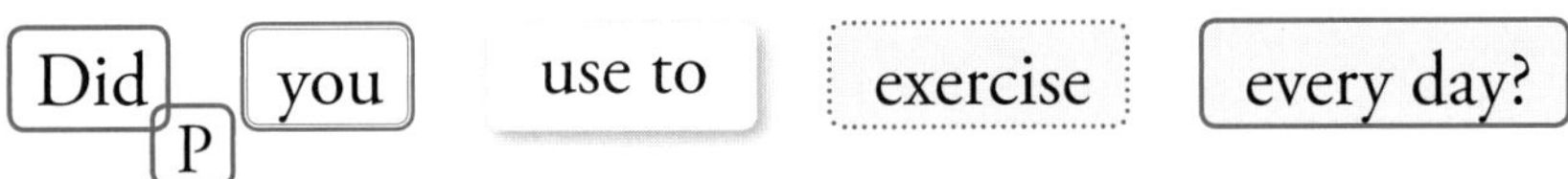

Negative Statements:

Note that for *yes/no* questions and negative statements, you must delete the *-d* in the word *used*.

ACTIVITY **J** Listen to the conversations. Write the habits that the speakers used to have.

CD 3 Track 8

Conversation 1. ______________________________

Conversation 2. ______________________________

Conversation 3. ______________________________

ACTIVITY **K**

1. Read the sentence beginnings and complete the sentences with a habit that you used to do at that time.

When I was little, ______________________________

Before I started this class, ______________________________

When I lived in my country, ______________________________

CD 3 Track 9

2. Listen to a student asking a classmate about habits she used to have.
3. Go around the classroom and find someone who had at least one habit in the past that was similar to yours. Make sure to use the speaking strategies you have already learned.

PRONUNCIATION

Pronouncing *-ed*

CD 3 Track 10

There are three possible sounds for the *-ed* ending of regular past tense verbs: /d/, /t/, and /ɪd/. If you don't pronounce the end of regular verbs correctly, your listener may misunderstand what you are trying to say. Use your tip of your tongue to pronounce regular past tense verb forms. Touch the tip of your tongue to the top of your mouth. Touch the bump right behind your front teeth.

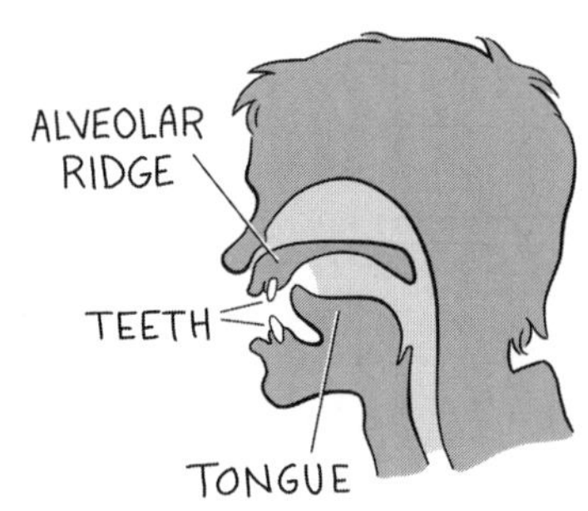

Pronouncing *-ed* as a /t/

If a verb ends in a voiceless sound, *-ed* will be pronounced as /t/. When you produce voiceless sounds, your vocal cords don't vibrate. Put your hand on your throat and say these sounds: /p/, /k/, /f/, /s/, *sh*, and *ch*. You should not be able to feel any vibrations.

ACTIVITY L

CD 3 Track 11

1. Listen and raise your hand when you hear a verb in the past tense.
2. Your instructor will point at different students. Be ready to pronounce the past tense forms of the verbs when he or she points at you.

a. watched	g. stopped
b. touched	h. mopped
c. laughed	i. kissed
d. stuffed	j. missed
e. walked	k. washed
f. talked	l. brushed

PRONUNCIATION

Pronouncing *-ed* as /d/

CD 3 Track 12

All of the regular past tense verbs that end in voiced sounds are pronounced /d/. When you produce voiced sounds, your vocal cords vibrate. Put your hand on your throat and say these sounds: /l/, /r/, /m/, /n/, /u/, /y/, /b/, /v/, and /z/. You should be able to feel vibrations.

ACTIVITY M

CD 3 Track 13

1. Listen and raise your hand when you hear a verb in the past tense.
2. Your instructor will point at different students. Be ready to pronounce the past tense forms of the verbs when he or she points at you.

a. prepared	g. harmed
b. listened	h. received
c. combed	i. used
d. studied	j. called
e. reviewed	k. happened
f. arrived	l. starred

PRONUNCIATION

Pronouncing *-ed* as /ɪd/

CD 3 Track 14

If a verb ends in a /d/ or /t/ sound, you have to make an /ɪd/ sound. Put your hand on your throat and say /ɪd/. You should feel your throat vibrate. When you say the /ɪd/ sound, stop the /d/ sound quickly.

ACTIVITY N
CD 3 Track 15

1. Listen and raise your hand when you hear a verb in the past.
2. Your instructor will point at different students. Be ready to pronounce the past tense forms of the verbs when he or she points at you.

a. traded	**g.** needed
b. started	**h.** reacted
c. waited	**i.** repeated
d. nodded	**j.** hesitated
e. graded	**k.** tested
f. wanted	**l.** painted

ACTIVITY O
CD 3 Track 16

Listen to the verbs. Put a check mark ✓ in the correct column to mark the sound you hear.

	/d/	/t/	/ɪd/
1. missed			
2. prepared			
3. asked			
4. permitted			
5. handed in			
6. washed			
7. failed			
8. visited			
9. excused			
10. completed			

ACTIVITY P

Work with a partner. Sit facing your partner. Say the verbs below in the present or past tense. Your partner will listen and identify what tense you are saying. Make sure to touch your tongue to the top of your mouth to make the /d/, /t/, or /ɪd/ sounds when you pronounce the verbs in the past tense.

miss	prepare	ask
permit	hand in	wash
fail	visit	excuse

PRONUNCIATION

Pronouncing *Used* To

CD 3 Track 17

When we pronounce the expression *used to*, we make it sound like one word—*uzta*. This pronunciation is the same for affirmative, negative, and interrogative forms.

ACTIVITY Q

CD 3 Track 17

Listen to the sentences. Circle the number that corresponds to the sentences where *uzta* is being used.

1 2 3 4 5 6 7 8 9 10

SPEAKING STRATEGIES

Self-Monitoring Your Speech

CD 3 Track 18

When you speak, it is important to pay attention to the language you are producing. This technique is called *self-monitoring* and can be used to correct your errors in speaking as you hear them. You can often self-monitor for the verb tense you are using. If you are speaking about the past, you need to self-monitor for past tense verbs. You can always correct yourself by using *I mean* and following this expression with a correction.

Listen to the example:

A: Hi, there. What's up?
B: Nothing special. How're you?
A: Good, good . . . So, how was your weekend?
B: It is, **I mean**, it **was** pretty good.
A: Uh-huh?
B: It was my father's birthday on Sunday.
A: Oh, I see.
B: Yeah, and the party is, **I mean** . . . **was** at my house.
A: Oh, yeah? I hope your father was happy.
B: Yeah, he was really surprised and excited!

ACTIVITY **R** Underline the instances of self-monitoring in this conversation between two international students.

A: So, I wanted to ask you . . . when . . . I mean, what are you going to do for spring break?

B: Oh. I'm not quite sure yet.

A: Really?

B: I, uh . . . I spent . . . I mean, I used to spend spring break with Dad, but, uh, . . . this year he's on vacation in Thailand.

A: Cool!

B: So, I guess I don't know.

A: Oh. Well, did, I mean, do you want to come over? I'm gonna barbecue.

B: Sounds great!

REVIEW AND EXPAND

ACTIVITY **A**

1. Work with a partner. You have two minutes to write requests for help that you would ask different people. For example:

   Ask a Friend: Could you please help me move on Friday?

   Ask a Classmate: Can you help me with the homework? I didn't understand the assignment very well.

   Ask your Father: Would you hang this picture on the wall for me?

2. Your instructor will ask you to choose one of the requests you wrote down. You and your partner have to write three excuses for why you can't do the favor. Write one excuse in the past tense, one in the present tense, and one in the future tense. Try to use adverbs of time in all of your requests. For example:

   Request: Could you please help me move on Friday?

Present	Past	Future
I'm so sorry, but on Friday afternoons, I have a class.	I'm very sorry. My mom asked me if I can drive her to the doctor's on Friday.	I'd love to, but I am going to visit my grandmother this Friday.

3. Write a suggestion to go along with each of your excuses. For example:

Present	Past	Future
I'm so sorry, but on Friday afternoons, I have a class. <u>I can help you after class.</u>	I'm very sorry. My mom asked me if I can drive her to the doctor's on Friday. <u>I could help you on Saturday.</u>	I'd love to, but I am going to visit my grandmother this Friday. <u>I can come to your place to help you unpack on Saturday.</u>

4. After you write, your instructor will ask you to exchange papers with another group. Read what the other group wrote and mark any errors in tense that you see.

ACTIVITY B

1. Work in pairs. You have to find as many similarities and differences as possible between habits you and your partner used to have when you were children. Write down the differences and similarities in the chart below.

Similarities	Differences

2. Share your list with your classmates. Refer to the Useful Expressions below to help you.

Useful
Expressions

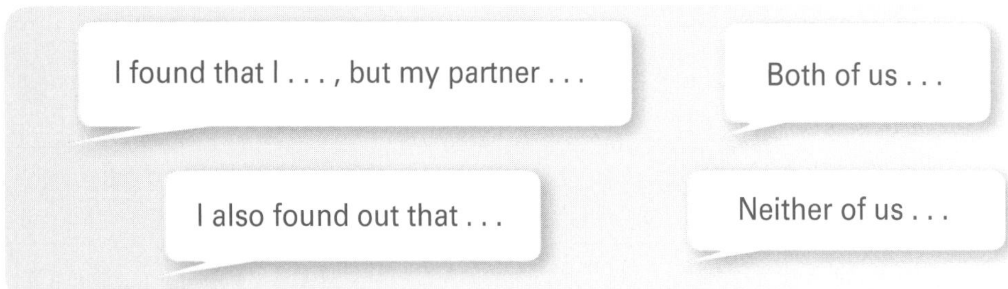

I found that I . . . , but my partner . . .
Both of us . . .
I also found out that . . .
Neither of us . . .

EVALUATION

ACTIVITY **A** Now that you have completed the activities in this chapter, complete the self-evaluation checklist below. Discuss your checklist with a classmate.

Self-Evaluation Checklist

- ☐ I used the simple past correctly.
- ☐ I used *used to* to discuss past habits.
- ☐ I listened for adverbs of time to help determine verb tense.
- ☐ I pronounced *-ed* endings correctly.
- ☐ I used encouragers in my conversations.
- ☐ I self-monitored my speech.

ACTIVITY **B** Look back at the chapter and the self-evaluation checklist above. What can you do this week to improve the skills you have learned in this chapter? Talk with a partner and write an action plan for how you can improve your skills this week.

Example *Sometimes I don't always pronounce verbs in the past tense correctly, so I'm going to self-monitor for that. Every time I talk, I will pay attention to the endings of the verbs in the past.*

Action Plan

CHAPTER

8 | Tell Me a Little about Yourself.

GET STARTED

ACTIVITY A
CD 3 Track 19

Listen to a student interviewing for a job on campus. What requests for information does the interviewer make in each part of the conversation? Write *1*, *2*, *3*, or *4* next to the sentence you hear in each conversation part.

_______________ Can you tell me about your responsibilities at your last job?

_______________ Did you have any trouble finding the office?

_______________ What is your greatest strength?

_______________ So, tell me a little about yourself.

ACTIVITY B
CD 3 Track 20

Listen to one interviewer talking to another student who wants a job at the campus pizza restaurant. Number the past events the student talks about in the order they are mentioned.

_______________ I came to the United States when I was 18.

_______________ I've never worked in a cafeteria.

_______________ I applied to college.

_______1_______ I was born in Mexico.

_______________ I've waited tables.

_______________ I studied for the GED last year.

> *GED* stands for *General Equivalency Diploma*. People who have not completed high school can take classes to prepare for the GED test. After they pass the test, they recieve a certificate that is equivalent to a high school diploma.

Cultural Note During a job interview, you should be sure to use polite and formal speech. It is OK to use hesitations, encouragers, and other speaking strategies during a job interview. However, you should make sure that you are always speaking formally by avoiding too many reductions and everyday expressions. If you speak too informally during an interview, it may be considered impolite.

ACTIVITY C The verbs in the chart below describe someone's job experience. Which of the verbs do you know? Imagine you want to use these verbs in an interview. Use a dictionary to look up any words that you do not know. Then match each sentence opener to the phrase that completes the sentence. More than one answer is possible.

Sentence Openers	Phrases
1. I restocked ______	a. the library books.
2. I counted ______	b. the shelves.
3. I handled ______	c. customer questions about the food.
4. I took ______	d. three classes last semester.
5. I reshelved ______	e. customer problems.
6. I answered ______	f. the money.
7. I filled ______	g. the files in the office.
8. I organized ______	h. orders from customers.

ACTIVITY D
CD 3 Track 21

1. Listen to two students discussing some common questions that interviewers ask.
2. Work with a partner and discuss the questions below. Refer to the Useful Expressions on the next page to help your discussion.
   a. What can you talk about when a job interviewer says, "So, tell me about yourself."?
   b. What were your responsibilities at your last job (including volunteer work, work at home, or responsibilities as a student)?

Useful
Expressions

I was born in . . .

I also had to . . .

I worked as a (job title) . . .

Let me see . . .

I was responsible for (verb + *ing*) . . .
(Example: I was responsible for answering the phone.)

LEARN AND PRACTICE

REVIEW: GRAMMAR

Yes/No Questions with Simple Past

Yes/no questions in simple tenses always use *do* as an auxiliary. If the question is in the simple present, the auxiliary *do* is used in the present. If the question is in the simple past, we use the past tense of *do*, which is *did*. You can use the sentence order below to help you make *yes/no* questions in the simple past tense.

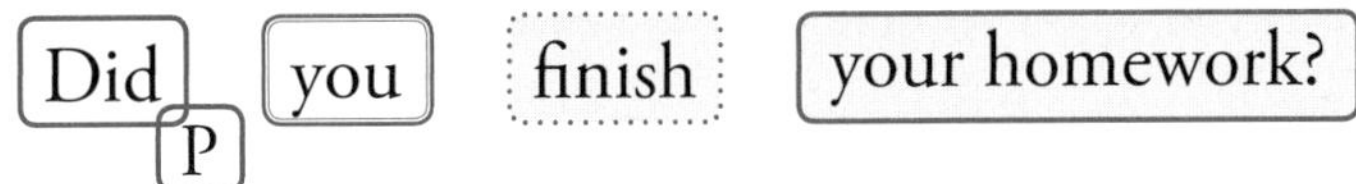

ACTIVITY **A**

1. Each student will write an on-campus job title on a sheet of paper and hand it to the instructor. One student will be chosen to go to the front of the classroom. The instructor will assign one of the on-campus jobs to the student at the front of the classroom. The student will imagine that he or she had that job last year.
2. The other students in the classroom will divide into two teams: Team A and Team B. Each team will take turns asking *yes/no* questions in the simple past to guess what the job was. The student who is at the front of the classroom can only answer *yes* or *no*. The first team to guess the job correctly wins a point. Use the examples below to help you think of more *yes/no* questions in the simple past.

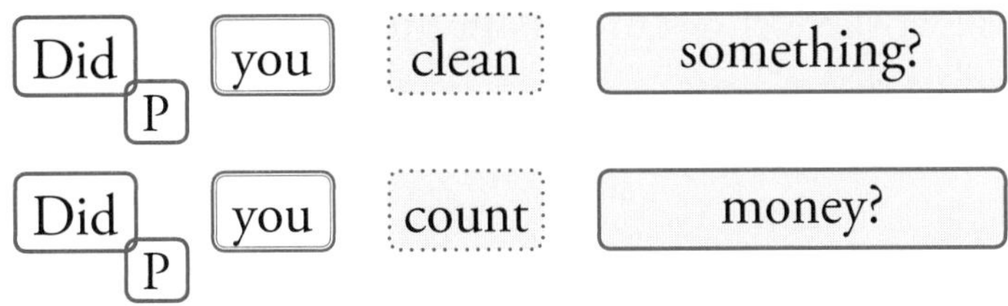

GRAMMAR

Wh- Questions with Simple Past

We can also ask questions in the simple past tense with *wh-* words, such as *when, what, where, who, why,* and *how.* All we need to do is to add the *wh-* word before *did.* Look at the examples below.

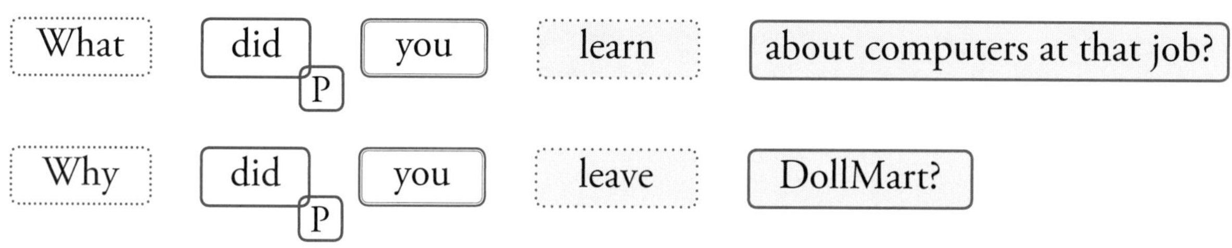

ACTIVITY **B**

1. Work in groups of three. You instructor will post large sheets of paper on the walls around the classroom. Your group will go to one of the sheets of paper. (Take a marker and a dictionary with you.) Your instructor will write a sentence about a past event on the board. Each group has two minutes to write as many *wh-* questions about that event as they can. Remember that your questions should be in the past tense.

Example

Sentence: I went shopping yesterday.

Questions: Where did you go?
What did you buy?
How much money did you spend?

2. After two minutes, move to your right and read the other group's questions. Do the questions make sense? Is the grammar correct? Give the group one point for each correct question. The group with the most points wins.

GRAMMAR

Talking about Past Experiences Using the Present Perfect

When we talk about experiences that happened in the past, but we do not give a specific time frame for when they happened, we use the present perfect tense. For example:

I | have | worked | in restaurants before.

The speaker has worked in restaurants in the past, but it is not clear when the speaker worked in restaurants.

(continued)

GRAMMAR (*continued*)

The form of the present perfect is different from the other verb forms we have studied so far because it requires two words. To talk about a past experience we have had using the present perfect, we need to use *have* as an auxiliary verb along with the past participle of the main verb. Look at the examples below.

I	have	waited	tables in three different cities.
I	have	worked	with children and adults.
I	have	worked	for admission offices in various colleges.

If the subject is *he*, *she*, or *it*, use *has*.

She	has	worked	for admission offices in various colleges.

ACTIVITY **C** Look at each person's job experience and the subject in parentheses. Write a sentence using the present perfect tense to describe each person's job experience.

Example **Experience:** work in construction (I)
Sentence: I have worked in construction.

a. Experience: play the guitar in bands around town (She)
Sentence: ______________________________

b. Experience: teach elementary school children (I)
Sentence: ______________________________

c. Experience: tutor for teenagers and adults (He)
Sentence: ______________________________

GRAMMAR

Questions in the Present Perfect Tense

To form questions in the present perfect tense, invert the auxiliary verb and the subject.

Have | you | worked | for a college before?

It is very common to use *ever* in questions in the present perfect tense. You should place this word after the subject of the sentence. For example:

Have | you | **ever** | worked | for a college before?

ACTIVITY **D** Write down three questions to ask your instructor about his or her past experiences. Be sure that your questions are in the present perfect tense.

a. Have you ever ridden a motorcycle?

b. ______________________

c. ______________________

d. ______________________

GRAMMAR

Negative Statements in the Present Perfect Tense

To form negative statements in the present perfect, we add *not* to the auxiliary verb *have*.

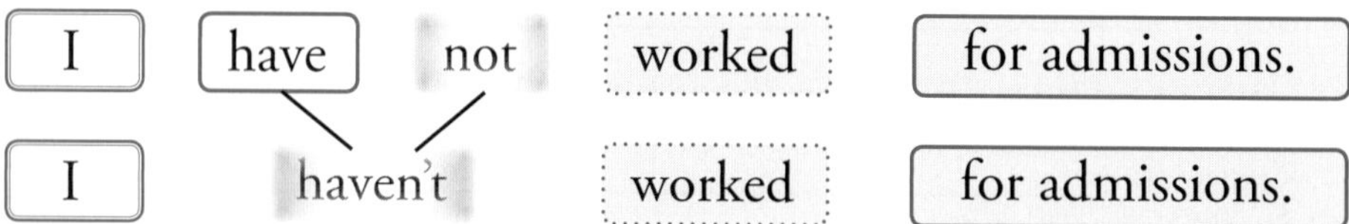

You can also use *never* instead of *not*. You cannot contract *never*, but you can contract *I have*.

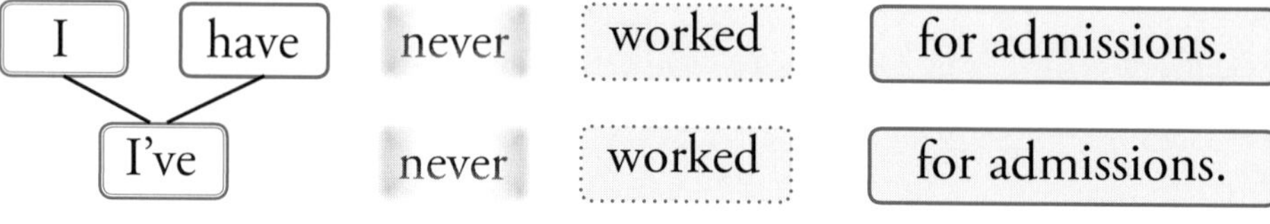

ACTIVITY **E** Write down three things you have never done but would like to do. Use *never* in your sentences and be sure that they are in the present perfect tense.

a. I've never flown in a helicopter. ______

b. ______

c. ______

d. ______

ACTIVITY **F** Write a question you would ask someone who is interviewing for the following jobs. Be sure to use the present perfect tense.

a. nurse ______

b. instructor's assistant ______

c. customer service representative ______

d. babysitter ______

e. administrative assistant ______

ACTIVITY **G** Listen to the conversation. Write the experiences the speaker has not had.

CD 3 Track 22

______

______

Cultural Note

The focus of a job interview is often work experience. You need to talk about your previous job responsibilities. If you don't have job experience, talk about your experience as a student or any volunteer or private work you have done, such as babysitting a younger sibling. Emphasize the qualities you have that will make you a good employee. It is not appropriate to talk about personal information such as age or marital status. Talk about your previous jobs, education, and hobbies or interests.

ACTIVITY **H**

1. Work in pairs. Student A is interviewing for a job. Student B is the interviewer. As a team, think of a job to apply for and write at least four questions that the interviewer might ask. Discuss the beginning and the end of the interaction and put everything together into a written script.

2. Practice the interaction from beginning to end without reading from the script. The script is just to help you compose the conversation. Student A should introduce himself or herself, answer Student B's questions, and end the interaction politely. Since you are not reading, your conversation will be different from the one you wrote on paper.

Remember to...

- use features of spoken language that you have already learned.
- hesitate.
- react.
- use sentence parts.
- use encouragers.
- ask for repetition when necessary.
- hedge.
- ask for clarification.

3. Pairs of students should present their dialogs to the class. Your dialog will be slightly different from the dialog you wrote in Part 1.

LISTENING STRATEGIES

Listening to Contextual Clues

Many times when we listen, we can make good guesses about the people and the events based on the words in the conversations, or contextual clues. Read the conversation:

A: Dude! Look over there!
B: Are they playing volleyball?
A: Yep. It looks like fun!
B: Yeah! Let's go ask if we can play.
A: Oh, no, wait. It looks like they are going towards the water.
B: Oh, yeah, the waves are getting bigger. Do you wanna go, too?
A: Well . . . it's cold!
B: Come on, man! Give me a break!

From the contextual clues in the conversation above, we can learn some information about who the speakers are and where they are located. We can probably guess that the speakers are at the beach because people are playing volleyball and swimming. Also, one of the speaker mentions the waves (in the ocean). The speakers are probably young men because one of them referred to the other one as *dude.* Also, one of them said, "Come on, man!"

Sometimes you have enough contextual clues to be sure something is true, but sometimes you do not have enough contextual clues to be certain. Then you can only make a good guess.

ACTIVITY **1** Work with a partner. Read the conversation below and look for contextual clues. With your partner, discuss and answer the questions that follow the conversation.

Interviewer: Can you tell me about your responsibilities at your last job?

Candidate: Well . . . I basically arrived in the morning and . . .um . . . because I was taking classes there at the college . . .

Interviewer: Uh-huh.

Candidate: In the afternoon, I . . . had to leave by 1:30 to . . . to go to class . . .

Interviewer: I see.

Candidate: So . . . the secretary always had a work assignment ready for me. Um . . . sometimes I filed things, and, um . . . sometimes I made copies.

Interviewer: Uh-huh.

Candidate: And . . . I . . . when the secretary went to lunch . . . I answered the phone and took messages.

Interviewer: I see. . . . OK, now . . . let's go to the next question.

Candidate: OK.

Interviewer: All right, then. . . What is your greatest strength?

Candidate: Um, let me see . . . well, I, um . . . I'm a very responsible person. I arrive on time for work . . . and I, um . . . do all my work very carefully. Uh, I remember one Friday . . . the secretary needed to leave early for spring break . . .

Interviewer: Uh-huh.

Candidate: So, she gave me an assignment, um . . . before she left . . .

Interviewer: Uh-huh.

Candidate: And I . . . I finished it and locked up the office.

Interviewer: Uh-huh.

Candidate: You know, um . . . even though I'm pretty young, I, um . . . I was trusted to do things correctly.

Interviewer: I see.

Candidate: Well, she knew how responsible I was.

Interviewer: Mm-hmm. Well, this job requires employees to be very responsible with money.

Candidate: Yes, I, um . . . imagine so.

Interviewer: Because . . . you need to count the money at the beginning and end of each shift.

Questions:

a. How old do you think the student is? How do you know?

b. What kind of job is this person applying for? How do you know?

c. Where was the student's previous job located? How do you know?

Cultural Note

When you go to a job interview, make sure that you are wearing appropriate clothing. No matter what job you are applying for, you should always appear to be professional. Don't forget to take extra copies of your résumé to your job interview.

CD 3 Track 23

Listen and write the correct answer to each question. Use the contextual clues you hear to help you answer.

A full-time job means one works about 40 hours a week and has benefits such as paid vacation time and health insurance. A part-time job means that one works less than 40 hours and often receives no benefits.

Conversation 1:

a. Is Omar a full-time student? What makes you think so?

____

b. Do you think he has children? How do you know?

____

c. What country does his sister live in? What makes you think so?

____

d. What kind of job is he interviewing for? How do you know?

____

Conversation 2:

a. Are the two people students? How do you know?

____

b. Is Marissa's job a full-time job? What tells you that?

____

The phrase "It's good money" means that a particular job pays well.

c. Was Chad's test hard? Why do you think that?

____

d. Does Chad still like video games? Why do you think that?

____

SPEAKING STRATEGIES

Asking for Clarification

Often, we can ask for repetition if we do not understand something. However, sometimes we do not understand the meaning behind a word or expression someone is using. If you do not understand something someone says, you can always ask him or her for a more detailed explanation. This strategy is called asking for clarification.

Ways of Asking for Clarification
What's . . . ?
What do you mean by that ? (formal)
What do you mean . . . ? (informal)
You mean . . .
I'm not sure I understand that word/expression . . .
I don't really know what you mean when you say . . .

Ways to Answer Clarification Questions
Let me see . . . how can I explain it . . . um . . .
What I mean is . . .
OK, um, it's a kind of . . .
Do you know what I mean?

It is acceptable to ask for clarification in a job interview. For example, you can say, "I'm really not sure I understand that word." The interviewer wants to communicate with you, and asking for clarification is a good strategy for having clear communication. Remember to use formal language during your interview.

ACTIVITY K Read the conversation between an instructor and a college student. Circle how the instructor asks for clarification and underline the student's answers to the questions.

A: Ms. Parker?

B: Hi, Andy. Come on in and have a seat . . .

A: Thank you.

B: You know, I like to talk to all my students at the beginning of the semester. . . . So, can you tell me a little about yourself?

A: Um, well . . . I was born and raised in Houston, Texas.

B: Houston, huh?

A: Mm-hmm. And . . . I'm a second-year student here at Gordon Community College.

B: OK, good. So what do you like to do in your free time?

A: Uh . . . I play soccer, and,um, some of my friends and I like to play "Go."

B: Oh, what do you mean by "Go?"

A: Let me see . . . how can I explain it . . . um, it's an ancient Chinese board game.

B: Oh, you mean it's a board game like checkers?

A: Mm-hmm. But it's more like chess.

ACTIVITY L Listen to the conversations. Complete the lines with the expressions you hear.

CD 3 Track 24

Conversation 1:

A: Hi, Ben.

B: Hi, what's up?

A: Nothing special. I started my volunteer job in the Students with Disabilities Office today.

B: Really? How's that?

A: It was good! I like it a lot.

B: So, what do you do there?

A: Um . . . sometimes I read for some of the students who are blind.

B: You do? Don't they have books on tape?

A: Uh, sometimes. And sometimes in Braille. But some books aren't on tape or in Braille, you know.

B: ______________________________ *Braille*?

A: You know what Braille is, right?

B: No. ______________________________

A: Oh. It's a kind of alphabet made with dots that you can touch . . . you know . . . for the visually impaired.

B: Oh, I see.

Conversation 2:

A: Hello, Ms. Goldberg. I'm here for my appointment.

B: Great, Vanessa. Please come in and sit down. . . You know I like to meet with all my students in the middle of the semester . . .

A: Uh-huh.

B: And . . . um . . . see how they're doing.

A: Ok.

B: So, how are things?

A: Pretty good actually. I do have one problem . . .

B: Mm-hmm?

A: Well, I um . . . I need to take a Level 5 writing class next semester . . .

B: Mm-hmm.

A: But they're all full already.

B: I see. Well, I teach the Level 5 hybrid class. Um . . .

A: ____________________________

B: It's a class that meets in the classroom part of the time, and you work on the computer the rest of the time.

A: Oh, ___________________ I have to have an Internet connection at home?

B: Uh-uh. You can go to the computer lab here, or a library, or someplace like that.

A: Um . . . ________________________________.

B: Well, let me show you the class syllabus . . .

Uh-uh is a very informal way of saying *no.*

PRONUNCIATION

Word Stress

Just as sentences have words that are stressed, *words* have *syllables* that are stressed. In most words, one syllable is stressed more than the others. Even if you pronounce the sounds that make up a word correctly, if you do not stress the correct syllable, people may have trouble understanding you. To stress a syllable, you need to pronounce the vowel in the syllable for a longer time. The syllable also needs to be louder. For example:

The word *produce* can be stressed in two different ways.

PROduce = vegetables and fruit

pro**DUCE** = a verb that means "to make"

In the question "Where is the produce aisle?", if *produce* is pronounced *proDUCE,* it will most likely cause misunderstandings.

ACTIVITY **M**
CD 3 Track 25

1. Look at the words below and say them syllable-by-syllable. Then listen and repeat after the speaker.

home·work	vol·un·teer	re·la·tion·ship	o·ver·a·chiev·er

2. Listen to the speakers. The speaker will first say *dah-dah* instead of the word. Listen for the longer vowel sound and higher voice in the stressed syllable. Then underline the stressed syllable in the word.

a. dah-dah planner
b. dah-dah-dah serious
c. dah-dah-dah-dah independent
d. dah-dah-dah-dah-dah overachiever

ACTIVITY **N**

1. How do you say the items below with correct word stress? Work with a partner. Face each other and pronounce the words below. Use "thumbs up" if your partner's pronounciation is correct and "thumbs down" if it is incorrect.

a. flexible
b. dependable
c. punctual
d. reliable
e. workaholic
f. a go-getter
g. a planner
h. a communicator
i. a team player
j. a perfectionist

A *go-getter* is a person who is ambitious, works hard, and takes action.

CD 3 Track 26

2. Listen to the audio to check your answers.

REVIEW AND EXPAND

ACTIVITY **A** Look at the verbs in each sentence. Decide if these verbs are in the present tense, the past tense, or the present perfect. Write *present*, *past*, or *present perfect* on each line.

Conversation 1:

Interviewer: Hello, how are you today? **1.** ____________

Ming-Lung: I'm fine, thank you.
How are you? **2.** ____________

Interviewer: Good. Please sit down.
Did you have any trouble finding our office? **3.** ____________

Ming-Lung: No. The office wasn't too hard to find. **4.** ____________

Interviewer: Good, good. So, tell me about yourself. **5.** ____________

Ming-Lung: Well, let's see . . . I was born and raised in Taiwan. 6. ______________

And I graduated from high school and college there. 7. ______________

I've worked in a lawyer's office before. 8. ______________

It's really interesting to work in a busy office. 9. ______________

Conversation 2:

Interviewer: Can you tell me about your responsibilities at your last job?

Holly: Well, I'm a student, so my job experience is all volunteer. 1. ______________

I worked for a blood drive on campus. So, um, I was responsible for setting up the signs and the table. 2. ______________

Interviewer: I see. 3. ______________

Holly: Yes, and I needed to greet students, and then I helped them sign up for a time to give blood. 4. ______________

Interviewer: Mm-hmm.

Holly: I sat at the blood drive tables for three days and helped sign up over two hundred people . . . 5. ______________

I think blood drives are really important for the community. 6. ______________

Conversation 3:

Interviewer: So, what's your greatest weakness? 1. ______________

Alex: Well, I'm a bit of a perfectionist. I always like to do things really well . . . so I work really carefully. 2. ______________

Interviewer: I see.

Alex: But I know that I need to pay attention to deadlines, so 3. ______________

I've started to set time limits for myself. 4. ______________

Interviewer: All right, thank you. So, let's go on to the next question. What would you say is your greatest strength?

Alex: Well, I'm a good communicator. Even though English is not my first language, people often ask me questions when they need help at work. Uh, I remember last year when my boss was sick, he left early and asked me to handle any problems that came up.

5. ____________

6. ____________

7. ____________

ACTIVITY **B** **1.** Read the three common interview statements and questions in the chart. Think about how you would respond to each of these statements and questions and write your answer in the chart below. Refer to the Useful Expressions to help you with your answers.

Tell me a little about yourself.	What's your greatest strength?	What's your greatest weakness?
	(Include an example from a past experience.)	(Describe a weakness and explain how you are working on it.)

Useful
Expressions

I'm flexible / independent / hardworking / responsible / punctual / reliable.

I'm a little too . . . careful / hardworking / quiet / independent / patient.

I'm . . . a planner / an organizer.

I'm a go-getter / a communicator / a team player.

I'm . . . a perfectionist / a workaholic.

I'm . . . a problem-solver / detail-oriented / dedicated.

2. Form two circles—an outside circle and an inside circle—with equal students in each one. Each student in the outside circle must stand facing a student in the inside circle. The students on the inside circle will ask one of the three questions from the chart on the previous page. Students on the outside circle will answer the question. Remember to self-monitor for correct verb tense and ask for clarification if you need to.

3. When your instructor says, "Switch roles," the students in the outside circle will ask their partner one of the three questions. Repeat the process until everyone has asked and answered all three of the questions.

ACTIVITY C

1. Work with a partner. Choose an job that students often have, such as a cashier, a restaurant worker, an office assistant, a library worker, a computer lab assistant, or a campus security guard. One student is the interviewer, and the other is the job candidate.

CD 3 Track 27

2. Listen to two students simulating an interview. Then begin your interview. Interviewers may choose to ask some of the questions from the chart below or they can come up with their own questions. Remember to self-monitor for word stress and tense. Ask for clarification if you need to. Make sure your partner uses appropriate language for an interview.

Starting questions:
1. How are you?
2. Did you have trouble finding our office?
3. How do you like the weather?
Questions about Experience:
4. Can you tell me about your work experience?
5. What job responsibilities did you have at your last job?
6. What's your greatest strength?
7. What's your greatest weakness?
Ending questions:
8. Do you want to work part-time or full-time?
9. Do you have any questions for me about the job?
10. When can you start work?

3. After you finish your first simulation, change partners and do a new interview.

EVALUATION

ACTIVITY **A** Now that you have completed the activities in this chapter, complete the self-evaluation checklist below. Discuss your checklist with a classmate.

Self-Evaluation Checklist

- ☐ I used the simple past tense correctly.
- ☐ I used the present perfect correctly.
- ☐ I asked for clarification when necessary.
- ☐ I used encouragers while speaking.
- ☐ I listened for contextual clues.
- ☐ I stress the correct syllables of words.
- ☐ I used more formal language in interview situations.

ACTIVITY **B** Look back at the chapter and your answers to the self-evaluation questions checklist above. What can you do this week to improve the skills you have learned in this chapter? Talk with a partner and write an action plan for how you can improve your skills this week.

Example *I really need to work on my job interview skills. I'm going to practice them with a tutor and with my neighbor. She speaks excellent English! I will come up with answers to the common interview questions and practice answering them. I'll look for more interview questions on the Internet. I'll also practice in front of a mirror once a week.*

Action Plan

CHAPTER

9 | What Are You Going to Do Next Weekend?

GET STARTED

CD 3 Track 28

1. Listen to one student tell another student about a future invention that she would like to have.
2. Look at the pictures below. Work with a partner and discuss what you see in the pictures. What kind of future inventions or innovations do you see? Would you like these inventions? How far off in the future are they?

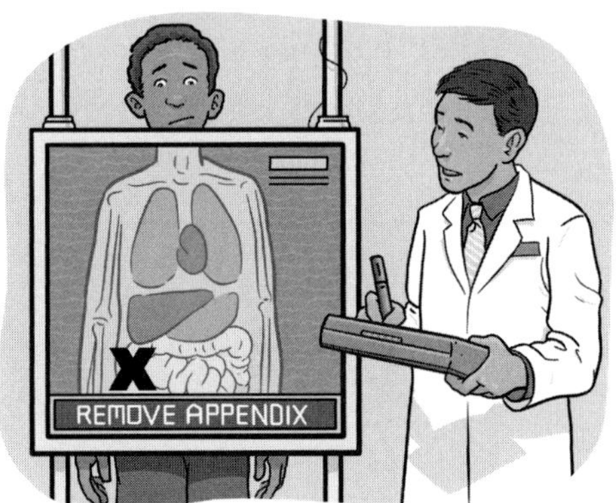

3. What other future inventions or innovations would be useful? Brainstorm a few ideas with your partner and share them with the class.

LEARN AND PRACTICE

GRAMMAR

Talking about Future Possibilities

We can talk about future possibilities in four different ways:

1. We can use *be going to* to talk about things that **are already changing**.

Computers | are going to | be | in every classroom.

2. We can use *will* to talk about things that **are possible**.

3. We can use *may* and *might* **for weaker possibilities**, or possibilities that could happen but are not very likely to happen.

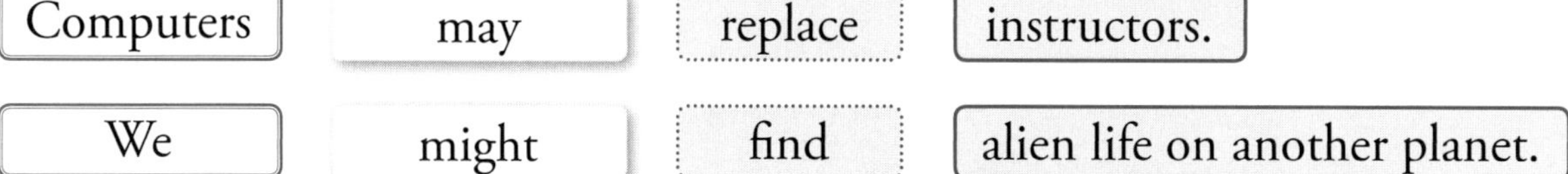

Computers
may
replace
instructors.
We
might
find
alien life on another planet.

4. We can use *won't* or *will never* for things that **are not possible to happen**.

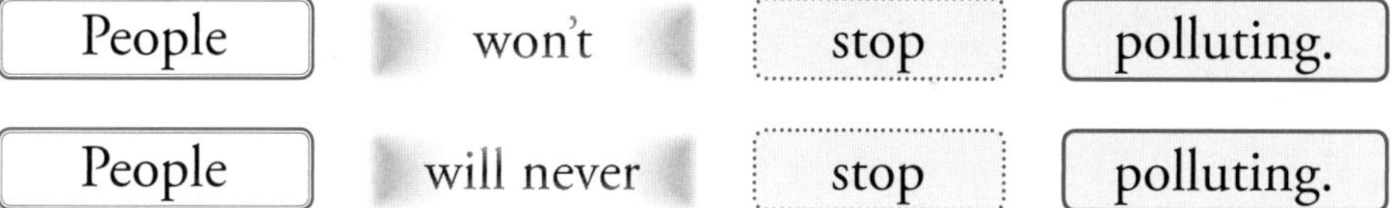

People
won't
stop
polluting.
People
will never
stop
polluting.

Look at the scale below to see how we can express different kinds of future possibilities.

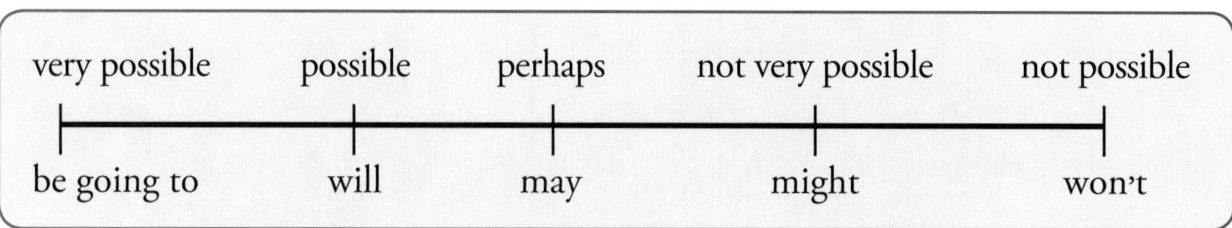

In English, there are many verbs that behave like modals. They are called *semi-modals*. Semi-modals are very common in conversational English. *Be going to* is a semi-modal, whereas *may*, *might*, and *will* are modals.

ACTIVITY **A** **1.** Read the sentences below about what transportation, housing, and education will be like in the future. Complete each sentence with the word that best represents what you think. You may use each word more than once. Look at the scale on page 142 to help you.

be going to	will (never)	may	might	won't

a. We ________________ drive flying cars.

b. Polar bears ________________ be extinct.

c. We ________________ all live to be 100 years old or older.

d. There ________________ be no more diseases.

e. We ________________ be able to fly from New York to Paris in two hours.

f. We ________________ live in space.

g. We ________________ only eat artificial foods.

h. There ________________ be printed newspapers.

i. There ________________ be rainforests.

j. We ________________ be able to teleport.

CD 3 Track 29

2. Listen to a group of three speakers discussing their answers to the first item. Work in groups of three and discuss your own answers.

GRAMMAR

Talking about Future Plans

We can talk about future plans and events in three different ways:

1. We can use *be going to* for **plans we have already made.**

I	am going to	leave	for Japan on the twenty-second.

This means that you already have the tickets and the plans are made.

2. We can use *will* for **decisions we make on the spot.**

A: Would you like to study together for the test tonight?

B: Sure. | I | will | study | with you. What time? |

You didn't have any plans. You just made the decision at this moment.

(continued)

GRAMMAR (*continued*)

3. We can use *may* or *might* for things **we're not sure we will or can do.**

I don't know if I can study with you tonight because . . .

I	may	have	to babysit my little brother.

I can't tell you now if I can come to lunch tomorrow because . . .

I	might	have	to take my mother to the doctor's office.

ACTIVITY **B** Look at the picture below. Complete the sentences with *will* or *be going to*. If the person has already made plans, use *be going to*, but if he or she is making a decision on the spot, use *will*.

a. I ________________ a soccer game tomorrow night. Would you like to come?

b. I ________________ go find a vase to put these flowers in.

c. I ________________ have some more fruit punch. Thanks.

d. I ________________ go get some paper towels to wipe up the spill.

e. I ________________ to leave for Italy tonight. I have to be at the airport in one hour.

f. I ________________ close the window for you.

ACTIVITY **C** **1.** Look at the list of ideas for plans you may have for next year. In front of each item, write *be going to, will, may, might,* or *will not.*

Next year, I . . .

a. ________________ travel to another country.

b. ________________ get a new job.

c. ________________ study more.

d. ________________ save money.

e. ________________ start exercising.

f. ________________ join a club.

g. ________________ learn a new skill.

h. ________________________________.
(your idea)

CD 3 Track 30

2. Listen to a group of students discussing their future plans. Stand up and move around the classroom. Talk to a classmate about his or her future plans and your own future plans. Then repeat the exercise two more times with different classmates.

Cultural Note When you talk about your future plans, you should pay attention to what topics you speak about. You should avoid talking about very personal topics with people you are not very close to, such as your coworkers, boss, and casual acquaintances.

PRONUNCIATION

Reductions (Reduced Forms) with *Will*

CD 3 Track 31

When talking about future plans, the word *will* can be reduced in more informal situations. When people say *will*, it is often reduced to the /l/ sound. Listen and repeat each example after the speaker:

I'll = eye-l	She'll = she-l	We'll = weel
You'll = yull	He'll = heel	They'll = they-l

ACTIVITY D
CD 3 Track 32

Work with a partner. Say one of the sentences from the box below aloud. Your partner will monitor your pronunciation of *will*. Your partner will use a "thumbs up" if your pronunciation is correct or a "thumbs down" if it is incorrect. Then switch roles and repeat the exercise. Listen to the audio to check if your pronunciation is correct.

I'll drive to New Jersey.

She'll drive to Arizona.

He'll fly to Maine on vacation.

He'll fly to California on vacation.

You'll tour California on vacation.

We'll tour Florida on vacation.

They'll tour Florida on vacation.

PRONUNCIATION

Reductions (Reduced Forms) with *Going To*

CD 3 Track 33

When people say *going to,* they can use either the nonreduced or the reduced pronunciation. Compare the nonreduced pronunciation "I'm going to go" with the reduced pronunciation "I'm *gonna* go." In written language, *going to* is spelled as two words. In informal spoken language, we pronounce it as one word—*gonna*. Remember *gonna* is not a written word. Repeat each sentence below after the speaker on the audio.

Nonreduced: I'm going to visit Washington, D.C.
Reduced: I'm *gonna* visit Washington, D.C.
Nonreduced: She's going to visit Los Angeles.
Reduced: She's *gonna* visit Los Angeles.
Nonreduced: You're going to go to Houston.
Reduced: You're *gonna* go to Houston.
Nonreduced: We're going to take a trip to Bangladesh
Reduced: We're *gonna* take a trip to Bangladesh.
Nonreduced: They're going to take a trip to Rio.
Reduced: They're *gonna* take a trip to Rio.

ACTIVITY **E** 1. Look at the pictures below. Luke already has plans for this weekend. Write a brief sentence for each picture telling what Luke is going to do. At least one sentence should be about what Luke is not going to do. Remember to use *is going to* or *is not going to* in every sentence.

2. Work with a partner. Use the sentences you wrote in Part 1 to discuss what Luke's plans are for the weekend. Say each of your sentences using the nonreduced form of *going to*. Then say the sentence again using the reduced form *gonna*. Your partner will monitor your pronunciation and correct it if necessary.

a. ______________________

c. ______________________

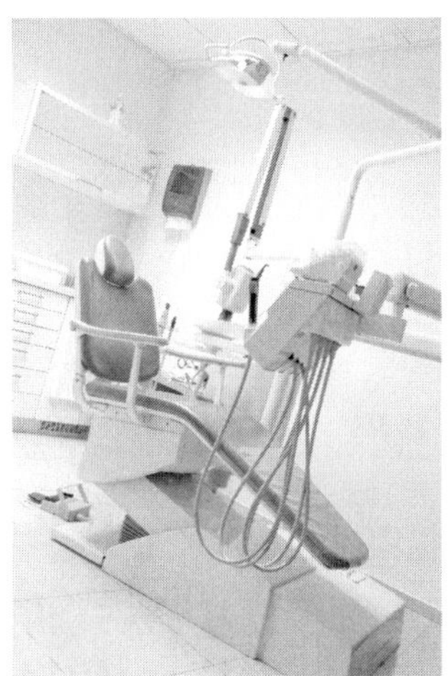

b. ______________________

d. ______________________

ACTIVITY **F**
CD 3 Track 34

1. Listen to two students discussing their plans for next year.
2. Work in groups of four. Discuss your plans for next year and find out if anyone in your group has some of the same plans you do. Refer to the Useful Expressions on the next page to help your conversation.

Remember to . . .

- use *be going to* for those things you think are already happening.
- use *will* for those things you think are very likely to happen in the future.
- use *may* and *might* for those things that are not very likely to happen in the future.
- use *will not* for those things you think are not likely to happen at all.
- react and use encouragers as you listen to the people in your group.

Useful
Expressions

- I think I'm going to . . .
- I have a good reason to...
- I know it's gonna be hard, but I . . .
- I think I'm going to have fun if I . . .
- You're really going to . . .?

REVIEW: LISTENING STRATEGIES

Understanding Main Ideas

In Chapter 5, you were introduced to a listening strategy that asked you to build mental pictures. You build mental pictures when your purpose is to understand the general information and main idea of what you are listening to, not the details. Remember that while you are listening, you should create a mental picture of what you hear and visualize the events as if you were making a movie.

1. Listen for the main ideas in each conversation. Put an *X* under "Made Plans" if the plans have already been made or put an *X* under "Possibility" if the speaker is still thinking about it.

Conversation 1	Made Plans	Possibility
a. go on a trip to Washington, D.C.	X	
b. stay at a hotel and tour the city		
c. visit museums		
d. stay there for a few days		
e. fly back		

Conversation 2	Made Plans	Possibility
a. visit Seattle		
b. see New Orleans during Mardi Gras		
c. visit Hawaii		
d. stay in Hawaii for a couple of days		
e. go to Japan		

2. Discuss which conversation sounds less formal. How do you know? What informal language did you hear?

ACTIVITY **H** With a partner, discuss places that you want to visit in the future and what you want to do and see in those places. Self-monitor for correct use of the future tense with *will, be going to, may, might,* and *will not.* Remember if you have already made your plans, use *be going to.*

SPEAKING STRATEGIES

Connecting Thoughts

When we speak, we use certain words and phrases that connect our thoughts. We also connect our ideas in writing, but the way we connect our ideas when we write is different from the way we do it when we speak informally. There are two major differences in how we use connectors in written language and informal spoken language:

1. A lot of written connectors are different from those used in informal spoken language.
2. When we write, we can use these connectors only once in a sentence. When we speak, we use them as many times as we want.

Connecting Thoughts with *And*

We can use *and* when speaking to connect sentences and add ideas.

For example:

- Well, I'm taking this English class **and** a computer class **and** I wanna take some other classes.
- I might visit San Diego **and** see my grandmother . . . **and** from there I can go down to Mexico for the day **and** practice my Spanish a little.

(continued)

Connecting Thoughts with *And Then*

You can use *and then* when speaking to connect events that happen one after another in a time sequence.

For example:

- I registered for the class, **and then** I found out I didn't have enough money to take it, **and then** I had to use my credit card to pay for it.
- I'm going to ask Laura to marry me, **and then** we'll plan our wedding, **and then** hopefully we'll get married in early June.

ACTIVITY I CD 3 Track 36 Complete the conversation with *and* or *and then*. Then listen to the conversation and check your answers.

A: Kurt, what classes did you take last year?

B: Well, um, I took English 201 ________ (a) American history—that was the class with too many people in it. I had that class with Professor Tanaka.

A: Oh, I remember that class ________ (b) it was OK. What are you going to take next semester?

B: I'm gonna take business writing ________ (c) public speech class ________ (d) tennis class.

A: Uh-huh.

B: I'm gonna finish all the classes, ________ (e) I'm going to try to get into a university,

A: Sounds great!

B: ________ (f) I want to get a really good job working in hotel management.

SPEAKING STRATEGIES

Connecting Thoughts with *'Cause*

You can use the informal word *'cause* (*because*) to connect a result with its cause.

For example:

- I failed the exam '**cause** I missed too many classes.
- She screamed '**cause** she saw a mouse run under her bed!

Connecting Thoughts with *But*

You can use the word *but* to show a contrast, make an excuse, and argue.

- A contrast = My sister is slim, **but** I need to lose some weight.
- An excuse = I'd like to go to the movies with you, **but** I have to study for a test.
- An argument = I know why you lied, **but** you should tell him the truth. He'll understand.

Connecting Thoughts with *Though*

You can use the informal word *though* in ways similar to how you use *but*. *Though* is a softer, gentler word. *Though* can be used to show that you want to consider a point or you want to argue in a gentle way. *Though* is much more common in speech than *but*.

For example:

1. A point to consider:

   A: That art class we're taking is really great!
   B: It is fun. Are we really learning anything, **though**?

   A: Let's go to the cafeteria and get lunch.
   B: Is the food good today, **though**?

2. A gentle argument (usually used with a negative question):

   A: Florida is definitely the best place to live.
   B: Don't they have tornados in Florida, **though**?

   A: I think I want to go to college in Boston.
   B: Isn't the city an expensive place to live, **though**?

ACTIVITY J CD 3 Track 37

Fill in the blanks in the conversation with *'cause*, *but*, or *though*. Then listen to the conversation and check your answers.

A: So, Andy, how's your job going?

B: I don't know. I wanted to keep this job I have now ________(a) the money is good and the company is good, ________(b) I think I'll look for another job soon.

A: You like it there, ________(c).

B: Yeah, I know, it's a good job like I said, ________(d) the company isn't doing well ________(e) it's too small, and I really want a job where I can move up in the company and get more money, you know.

A: Yeah, yeah. I see what you're saying. Um, you said your boss is really kinda nice at the job you have now, ________(f).

B: Yeah. I'll really miss her. I have to do what is best for me, ________(g).

ACTIVITY K

Complete the conversation with the connectors *and*, *and then*, *'cause*, *but*, and *though*.

A: Phew! The semester is almost over!

B: Yep. Looking forward to my two weeks off.

A: Me, too. What are you going to do?

B: Um, well . . . I think I may take some days off work ________(a) go visit my aunt in Vegas.

A: Oh, that sounds fun!

B: Oh, yeah. ________(b) I want to drive to the Grand Canyon. Never been there.

A: Oh, really?

B: Uh-huh. I'm looking forward to it. It may be too expensive, ________(c).

A: Yeah, I tried going there once.

B: Uh-huh.

A: But I ended up not going ________(d) it was too expensive.

B: Oh, I see. Did you try to stay at a hotel?

A: Uh-huh.

B: Yeah. That can be a problem, ____________ I'm going to camp.
(e)

It's cheaper and kind of more of an adventure.

A: That's an adventure all right!

ACTIVITY **L** Work with a partner. Talk about your plans for when the semester is over. Make sure to use connectors in your conversation.

REVIEW AND EXPAND

ACTIVITY **A** Work with a partner. One student is Student A and the other is Student B. Have a conversation about your future travel plans. You should use the list of questions below to guide you through your conversation. You can also ask your own questions. Student A should begin the conversation and Student B should answer each question and follow the guide to respond.

Student A	Student B
1. Do you travel much? 3. Are you planning to take a trip anywhere in the near future? 5. Do you like traveling to new places, or are you more of a homebody who likes the comfort of home? 7. So, what do you think is the worst thing about traveling? 9. Are you going to do anything on your next trip to avoid that problem? 11. What's the worst problem you've heard of people having when they were on a trip, like losing their wallet or something? 13. OK, so what about great places? Are there any places that you dream of traveling to?	2. How about you? 4. So, those are my plans. What about you? Are you taking off for anyplace soon? 6. So, that's my story. Let me guess. You are more of a traveler/homebody. 8. So, what about you? Do you agree with me? 10. What is some advice you give people about traveling? 12. Are you going to do that on your next trip? 14. Are there any places you don't want to travel to 'cause you think they're dangerous?

Take off means to leave quickly.

Remember to . . .

- hesitate.
- ask for repetition.
- repeat words and questions for clarification.
- react.

ACTIVITY **B** Work in groups of three or four and talk about the questions below. Use all of the tenses and modals you have learned in your conversation. Refer to the Useful Expressions to help your discussion.

1. What can you do now that you couldn't do at the beginning of this course?
2. What things helped you learn the most?
   - Did you listen to the book's CD at home or in the lab?
   - How much did you study every week?
   - Did the listening strategies help you with your listening skills?
   - Did speaking English with your classmates make you feel more confident?
   - What other things do you think were helpful?
3. What things do you still have trouble with in English? Why? What can you do to improve those things?
4. What will you do in the future to continue improving your English?
5. What do you plan to do after you finish this class?

Useful
Expressions

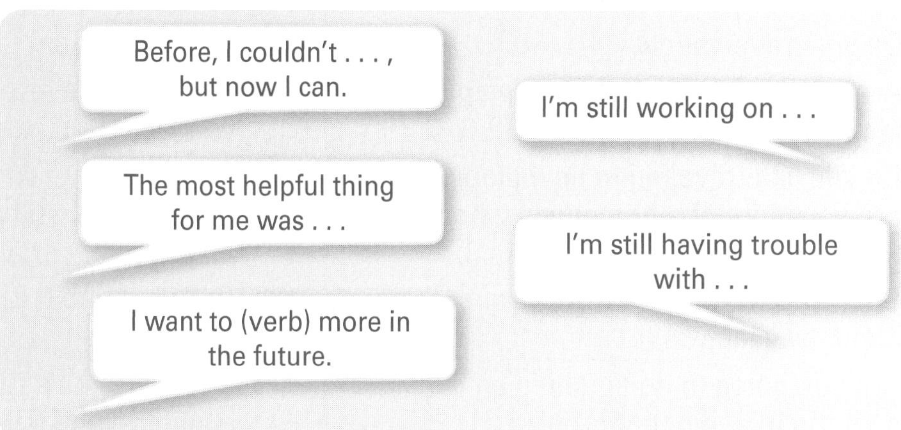

Before, I couldn't . . . , but now I can.
The most helpful thing for me was . . .
I want to (verb) more in the future.
I'm still working on . . .
I'm still having trouble with . . .

Remember to . . .

- use connecting words like *'cause, and, and then, but,* and *though.*
- self-monitor for correct use of past, present, and future verb tenses.
- use these expressions to talk about future plans: *I'm going to, I'll, I may, I might.*

EVALUATION

ACTIVITY **A** Now that you have completed the activities in this chapter, complete the self-evaluation checklist below. Discuss your checklist with a classmate.

Self-Evaluation Checklist

- ☐ I talked about future possibilities correctly.
- ☐ I talked about my future plans correctly.
- ☐ I correctly pronounced the reduced form of *will* and *going to.*
- ☐ I used connectors *and, and then, 'cause, but,* and *though.*
- ☐ I was able to listen for the main idea by creating a mental picture.
- ☐ I self-monitored for correct use of verb tenses.

ACTIVITY **B** Look back at the chapter and the self-evaluation checklist above. What can you do this week to improve the skills you have learned in this chapter? Talk with a partner and write an action plan for how you can improve your skills this week.

Example **When I talk about my future plans, I need to make sure I am using the correct modals. I'm going to practice talking about my future plans with my tutor at least once a week.**

Action Plan

CHAPTER 10

Would You Like to Come?

GET STARTED

ACTIVITY A

CD 3 Track 38

1. Listen to two people discuss one of the pictures below.
2. Work with a partner. Look at the pictures and discuss these questions: What do you see in the pictures? Where are the people? What are they doing? How often do you do these things?

CD 3 Track 39

3. Listen to six conversations. In each conversation, someone is being invited to do something. Number the pictures from 1 to 6 in the order you hear them. Remember to create mental pictures as you listen.

a. ______________________

d. ______________________

b. ______________________

e. ______________________

c. ______________________

f. ______________________

ACTIVITY **B** CD 3 Track 40

Listen again. One person in each conversation made an invitation. Did the other person accept the invitation, decline the invitation, or was he or she unable to give a definite answer? Put an *X* on the correct line below.

Conversation	Accepted	Declined	Not Sure
1	X		
2			
3			
4			
5			
6			

LEARN AND PRACTICE

GRAMMAR

Describing Activities with *Go* and *-ing* Action Verbs

When we want to talk about certain activities, we often use *go* and an action verb in the *-ing* form. We usually use *go* and an *-ing* action verb when we are talking about a physical activity. The use of *go* with an action verb usually indicates that you have to travel a short or long distance to do the activity. For example:

go swimming   go bowling   go shopping   go hiking

I wanna **go swimming** this weekend. Wanna join me?
I usually **go hiking** on the weekend. I love it!

Wanna is the reduced form of *want to*. This word is only used in spoken English; it is not used in written form.

ACTIVITY **A** Look at the action verbs in the box below. Write an original sentence for each verb using *go* and the *-ing* form of the verb.

ski	swim	hike	shop
dance	scuba dive	surf	bike

1. I'd love to go skiing this winter. I've never been before!
2. ______________________

3. ______________________________

4. ______________________________

5. ______________________________

6. ______________________________

7. ______________________________

8. ______________________________

GRAMMAR

Using Invitation Phrases

Often we want to invite people to do things with us. Some invitation phrases that you can memorize are given below. Once you have learned these invitation phrases, you can add the base form of the verb to create many different invitations.

For example:

Would you like to	go	dancing on Saturday?
Do you wanna	see	a movie tonight?
Let's	get	something to eat.

If you use *how about* to begin an invitation, the verb that follows needs to be in the *-ing* form.

How about	going	dancing on Saturday?

Cultural Note In North American culture, there are many different kinds of friendships. Some friendships last a lifetime and are very close. However, there are many other kinds of friendships. Often friendships are formed when two people do an activity together, such as taking the same class. People in this type of friendship do not often do other activities together, but they are still fond of each other and act in a friendly way when they see each other.

ACTIVITY **B** The words in the invitations below are not in the correct order. Put the words in the correct order and write the invitations on the lines. Be sure to use the correct punctuation at the end of each invitation.

Bungee jumping is an activity where you jump from a high place. You have a strong elastic rope and harness attached to you that springs back before you hit the ground.

a. have dinner together you do want to tonight

____

b like you to would with us salsa dancing go tonight

____

c. wanna you go bungee jumping do with me this weekend

____

d. go get let's some ice cream right now

____

REVIEW: GRAMMAR

Making Excuses Using the Present, Past, and Future Tenses

When you decline an invitation, it is polite to apologize and give an excuse. First, you must use an expression that indicates if you are accepting the invitation or declining the invitation.

Accepting the Invitation	Declining the Invitation
• Sure. That's a great idea.	• Sorry, I'd like to, but . . .
• Yeah, that sounds good.	• Oh, I'm sorry, I can't. I . . .
• Oh, sure. That sounds fun.	• Sorry, that sounds good, but I . . .

If you decline an invitation, you can give a more detailed explanation as to why you can't accept the invitation by using the present, past, or future tense in your excuse. For example:

Invitation: Would you like to have lunch together in the cafeteria after class?

Present: I'm sorry, I have lunch with my Dad on Thursdays.

Past: I'm sorry, Joe invited me to eat with him today.

Future: I'm sorry, I'm going to head home after class today.

You can also accept an invitation at the time of the invitation by using *will.*

Future: Sure, I will go with you.

ACTIVITY **C** Read the short conversations below. Are the excuses in the present, past, or future? Write your answer on the line next to each excuse.

Conversation 1:

A: Hi, Mary!

B: Hi, there.

A: Wanna go see a movie Friday after class?

B: Sorry, but I go to the gym every day after class. ______________

A: How about in the evening?

B: Sounds great.

Conversation 2:

A: Hey, Carol?

B: Yes?

A: Let's go get some coffee?

B: Sorry, I can't. I'm going to meet Steve in five minutes. ______________

Conversation 3:

A: John?

B: Hey, Dude.

A: Would you like to come to my place to watch the game?

B: This coming Sunday?

A: Uh-huh.

B: Sorry, Dude. Adam invited me to his place. ______________

ACTIVITY **D** The word *today* can be very tricky because it can refer to the past, present, or future. Read the sentences below. Use context clues and write if the word *today* is referring to the past, present, or future.

a. I woke up so tired today that I couldn't get out of bed. ______________

b. I'm going to start a new diet later today. ______________

c. Today people can communicate any time they want with the Internet and cell phones. ______________

d. I went to the grocery store earlier today. ______________

ACTIVITY **E** **1.** Think of something you want to invite your classmate to do later today. Write an invitation.

Invitation: ______________________________

2. Work with a partner. Exchange books with your partner. Read your partner's invitation and write down three excuses for why you have to decline the invitation: one in the present, one in the past, and one in the future.

   a. Excuse in the present: ______________________________

   b. Excuse in the past: ______________________________

   c. Excuse in the future: ______________________________

3. Return the book to your partner. Check the excuses your partner wrote. Discuss with your partner if the excuses are appropriate and grammatically correct.

CD 3 Track 41

1. Listen to one student inviting another student to do something.

2. Work with a partner. You and your partner are going to take turns inviting each other to do something. Accept or decline your partner's invitation. Be sure to give an excuse. Refer to the Useful Expressions below to help your conversation.

Useful ***Expressions***

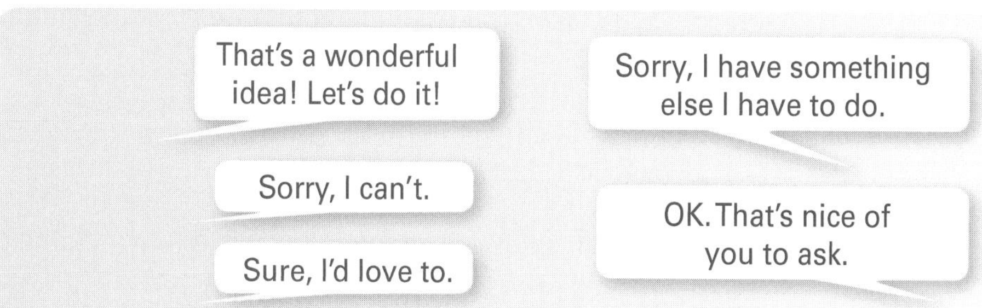

That's a wonderful idea! Let's do it!
Sorry, I have something else I have to do.
Sorry, I can't.
OK. That's nice of you to ask.
Sure, I'd love to.

REVIEW: GRAMMAR

Using Modals to Express Necessity, Obligation, and Promises

If you turn down an invitation, you can express necessity or obligation in your excuse. In Chapter 5, you learned how to express necessity and obligation. Let's review.

I	have to	run	errands this afternoon.
I	should	read	the chapter again before the test.
I	need to	go	home.
I	have got to	study	for my English exam.
I'm	supposed to	help	my little sister with her homework.

When you turn down an invitation, you can also promise to do what you are being invited to do some other time.

For example: I | will | go | with you tomorrow.

ACTIVITY **G** Read the conversation below. Circle the expressions of necessity or obligation and underline the promise.

A: Hey, Gil.
B: Hi.
A: Are you doing anything?
B: Not really. Just checking my e-mail. Why?
A: Well, would you like to go get some coffee at the new coffee shop?
B: Now?
A: Yes.
B: I need to finish checking my e-mails.
A: Oh.
B: I can go after that.
A: OK.
B: I'll see you there in about 30 minutes then.
A: OK.

ACTIVITY **H** Work with a partner. One of you will invite the other person to do something. The other person will turn down the invitation, express necessity or obligation, and then make a promise using *will*. After you have finished, switch roles and repeat the exercise.

GRAMMAR

Expressing Certainty and Uncertainty

In this book, you have learned how to express ideas in the present, past, and future. You have also learned how to use modals to express a variety of concepts. Now, let's learn how to express uncertainty—what we are not sure about. There are two ways of expressing uncertainty. One way is by using the modals *may* and *might*.
For example:

I	may	have to	work tomorrow.
I	might	go	to the beach this weekend.

Another way to express uncertainty is to use adverbs, such as *maybe* and *probably*. *Maybe* is usually inserted at the beginning of the sentence.

- **Maybe** I have to work overtime.

Probably is commonly used with *will*.

- I'll **probably** have to work on that day.

ACTIVITY **I** Work with a partner. Look at the underlined sentences and decide if the speakers are expressing certainty or uncertainty. Discuss with a partner how you chose your answer.

A: Hello.

B: Mary?

A: Hi, Desi. What's up?

B: I'm glad I caught you at home. Um . . . Beth just called . . .

A: Yeah?

B: And, uh . . . invited us to go spend the weekend with her at her beach house. Wanna go?

A: When would we leave?

B: I'm not sure. <u>We might leave Friday night if you are free.</u> (a)

A: Oh, um . . . sorry. <u>I've got a conference call Friday around six P.M.</u> (b)

B: Oh, no!

A: Yeah . . . one of those things, you know.

B: I know. How about Saturday?

A: Do you think Beth will be willing to wait until Saturday morning because of me?

B: <u>She might.</u> (c)

A: Um . . . well, <u>let's leave on Saturday then.</u> (d)

B: Cool! <u>I'm going to call her, and I'll call you right back to let you know.</u> (e)

A: All right, then.

B: Oh, I just remembered . . . she's working tonight.
<u>I'll probably wait until tomorrow to call her.</u> (f)

A: Oh, OK. Just call me tomorrow, then. No biggy.

> *No biggy* is a slang expression that means "no big deal" or "it's not very important."

ACTIVITY **J** **1.** Read the invitations and responses in the chart below. Match each invitation with the most appropriate response.

Invitation	Acceptance or Excuse
1. Would you like to go shopping with me sometime soon? ______	a. Oh, I'd like to, but I'm having lunch with someone else.
2. I want to see a movie this weekend. Would you like to go with me? ______	b. That's an excellent idea. We can help each other.
3. Hey, do you wanna study for the test together? ______	c. I usually work on Saturdays, but this coming Saturday I'm off. What do you wanna see?
4. Do you wanna go to the campus bookstore with me? ______	d. That's a good idea. I don't understand it, either.
5. Let's have lunch together in the cafeteria after class. ______	e. Maybe. Where do you like to go shopping?
6. Let's go ask the instructor about the homework. ______	f. Oh, I'd like to, but I already bought my books.

2. Read the responses again. Write if the person *accepted* the invitation, was *not sure*, or *declined* the invitation.

1. ______________________________

2. ______________________________

3. ______________________________

4. ______________________________

5. ______________________________

6. ______________________________

ACTIVITY **K** **1.** Write three things you would like to invite a classmate to do with you. Write the three invitations and where you want to do them on the lines below.

a. ______________________________

b. ______________________________

c. ______________________________

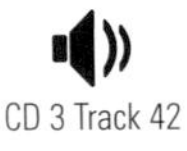

CD 3 Track 42

2. Listen to three examples of students inviting their classmates to do something with them. Then, look at your list from Part 1. Walk around the classroom inviting your classmates to do these things with you. They will also invite you to do things with them. Accept the invitations or turn them down using the present tense, past tense, or future tense. Make excuses that express necessity or obligation. Make promises for the future if you have to decline. Express uncertainty if you are not sure if you can accept the invitation. Refer to the Useful Expressions below to help you.

Useful
Expressions

Is anyone else going?
Yeah, that sounds good.
Sorry, I'd like to, but I have some stuff to do.
Oh, sure. That's an excellent idea.
Sorry, that sounds fun, but I have some things to do.

SPEAKING STRATEGIES

Talking around a Word

It is very common to forget how to say something. Talking around a word is a strategy used in speaking. When you talk around a word, you explain things that relate to the word you are thinking of, such as what it is made of, how you use it, etc. Talking around a word usually helps you think of the word that you have forgotten.

ACTIVITY **L** Listen to the examples of talking around a word. During the pause, write the word the person is talking around.

CD 3 Track 43

Conversation 1: ____________________

Conversation 2: ____________________

Conversation 3: ____________________

ACTIVITY **M** Work with a partner. Come up with an object that you need. You are going to talk around the word and ask for the object without saying its name. Your partner will guess the object. Then switch roles with your partner and repeat the exercise. Refer to the Useful Expressions below to help you.

Useful
Expressions

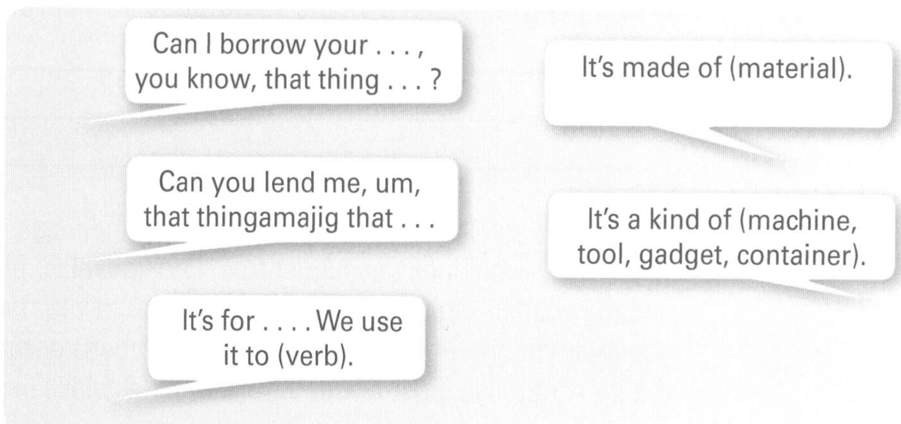

Can you lend me, um, that thingamajig that . . .
It's for . . . . We use it to (verb).
It's made of (material).
It's a kind of (machine, tool, gadget, container).

REVIEW: LISTENING STRATEGIES

Using Context Clues

In Chapter 8, you learned how to use context clues to help you understand main ideas. You can also listen for context clues when people are talking around a word. The context clues will help you understand the main idea, even if the speaker cannot remember the correct word to use.

ACTIVITY N
CD 3 Track 44

Listen to people asking to borrow some objects. Complete the sentences with the words you hear. Then you will hear a pause. Write the word the speaker is talking around. Listen to the rest of the conversation to check your answer.

Conversation 1:

A: Hi, Pat.
B: Hello, Jihung.
A: Can I borrow your, um . . . you know, that ______________ (a) you use to keep time.
B: I'm not sure I know what you're saying.
A: Uh . . . you know, that small gadget . . . it's a kind of ______________ (b). I wanna see how fast I can run . . .
B: Oh, I know, you mean my ______________ (c).
A: Yes, thanks.

Conversation 2:

A: Hey, what's new, Katie?
B: Nothing much, Arturo. What's up?
A: Could you give me a . . . um, it's a small thing. It's made of ______________ (d).
B: I don't know what you mean . . .
A: Let me think . . . um, it's for holding a few pieces of paper ______________ (e).
B: Hmmm . . .
A: I need it in order to keep these three pieces of paper together when I hand them in during class . . . to our instructor.
B: Oh! OK. . . . Let me give you a ______________ (f).

ACTIVITY **0** Work in groups of three. Look at the names of the objects in the box below. Imagine you need to borrow these objects but you cannot remember the word for them. Describe each object to the other members of your group by talking around the word. The group member who guesses the object correctly will choose a new object and repeat the exercise.

notebook	cell phone	dictionary
book	eraser	pencil
pen	calculator	(your own idea)

REVIEW: PRONUNCIATION

Stress and Reductions (Reduced Forms)

CD 3 Track 45

In this book, we have learned two important pronunciation concepts: stress and reduction (reduced forms). When we talk, we stress content words by making them louder and longer. We reduce the other words by making them shorter or by connecting them.

For example:

I want to go to the beach this weekend.

The content words are the ones that contain information. If we eliminate the non-content words, we can still understand the information.

I want __ go ___ ___ beach ______ weekend.

The stressed syllable of these content words is pronounced longer and louder. The non-content words are reduced. That means their vowels are reduced to a schwa /ə/. Instead of pronouncing *o*, *e*, or *i* we relax our tongue and produce a schwa. For example:

to = t/ə/ the = th/ə/ for = f/ə/r

Sometimes words are combined and sound like one word. For example:

I want to go to the beach this weekend.
want to = wanna

In casual conversation, the sentence sounds like this:

I wanna go t/ə/th/ə/ beach /th/ə/s weekend.

ACTIVITY **P** 1. Read the sentences and underline the content words.

a. I'd like to go to Cancún and stay at a nice hotel.

b. Nobody knows what is going to happen.

c. She's definitely getting a better job after she graduates.

d. They'll go if you ask them.

e. My husband said that he's going to a game on Sunday.

f. I want to study for the test tonight.

CD 3 Tracks 46

2. Listen to the sentences again and check your answers. Circle the reduced words.

3. Work with a partner. Sit facing each other. Pronounce the sentences. Your partner will correct you if your stress and reduction are incorrect. Switch roles.

ACTIVITY **Q** 1. Look at the list of places below. Think about and write what activity you are going to invite your friend to do there.

Place	Activity
a. circus	watch the jugglers
b. night club	___
c. dance school	___
d. museum	___
e. zoo	___
f. café	___
g. amusement park	___

CD 3 Tracks 47

2. Listen to someone inviting a friend to the circus. Work with a partner. You are going to invite your partner to go to one of the six other places from the list above. Pretend you don't know how to say the name of the place. Use the talking around a word strategy and let your partner guess the name of the place. Refer to the Useful Expressions below to help your conversation.

Useful
Expressions

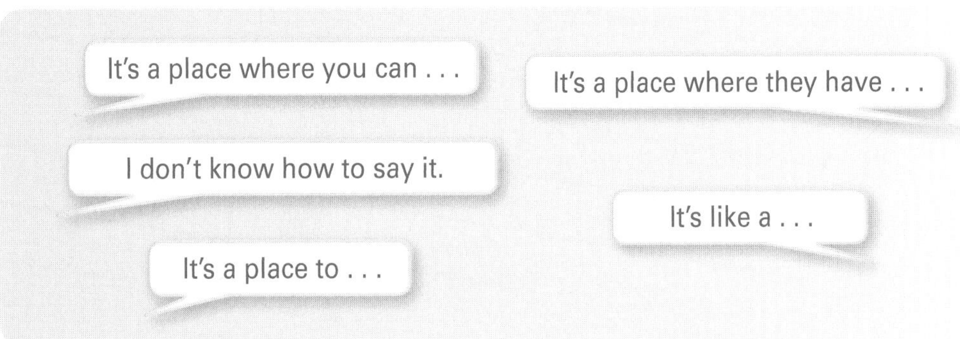

It's a place where you can . . .
It's a place where they have . . .
I don't know how to say it.
It's like a . . .
It's a place to . . .

REVIEW AND EXPAND

ACTIVITY **A** **1.** When someone invites you to do something, you often ask questions. What questions do you ask? Write them in the chart below.

Questions about the time	Questions about the place or activity	Questions about how to get there	Other questions
What time does it start? How long do you want to stay there?	How much does it cost? Do a lot of people go there?	Do we have to take the bus? How long does it take to get there?	Who else is going? Can I bring a friend?

2. Look at the schedule organizer below. Write down the times you work, go to school, or do other tasks. Then write down two things you want to do during your free time.

3. Divide the class into two lines: Line A and Line B. Each student in Line A will invite their partner to do something. Students in Line B will look at their schedule and accept or decline the invitation. When your teacher says, "Rotate," students in Line A will move one step to the right, and the student at the end of Line A will move to the beginning of the line. Repeat the activity until all students are facing the partner they started with.

EVALUATION

ACTIVITY **A** Now that you have completed the activities in this chapter, complete the self-evaluation checklist below. Discuss your checklist with a classmate.

Self-Evaluation Checklist

- ☐ I made invitations using correct grammar.
- ☐ I accepted and turned down invitations politely.
- ☐ I gave polite excuses when I turned down invitations.
- ☐ I used the present, past, and future tense correctly.
- ☐ I expressed certainty and uncertainty.
- ☐ I expressed necessity, obligation, and promise.
- ☐ I was able to talk around a word.
- ☐ I emphasized important words with sentence stress.
- ☐ I reduced non-content words.
- ☐ I listened for context clues.

ACTIVITY **B** Look back at the chapter and the self-evaluation checklist above. What can you do this week to improve the skills you have learned in this chapter? Talk with a partner. Turn to the next page and write an action plan for how you can improve your skills this week.

Example *I always expect people to pronounce every word clearly. Reductions are difficult for me, so I'm going to do listening exercises and practice identifying reductions. I will also work on pronouncing words with the schwa. I need to pronounce the syllables of non-content words with a schwa. I will practice this every day for about ten minutes and pay attention to schwas when I am talking.*

Action Plan

PHOTOCOPIABLE MATERIALS

CHAPTER 2

REVIEW AND EXPAND

ACTIVITY B PAGE 29

STUDENT 1: THE CLERK

Look at the map of the store below. Look at the items on the list. Choose a location for each item on the list and draw it in the map. The customers will ask where certain items are located in the store. Look at your map and give the customers directions to each item.

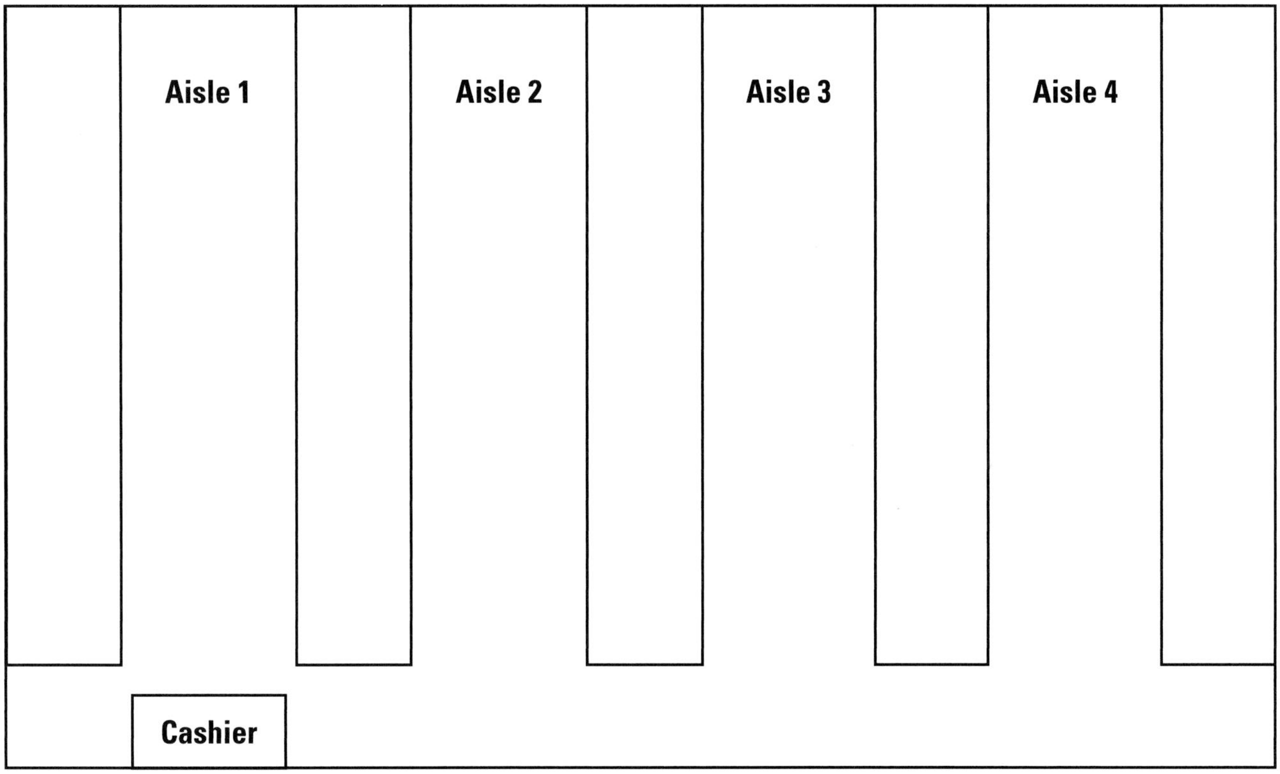

	Aisle 1		Aisle 2		Aisle 3		Aisle 4	
	Cashier							

Items:

cosmetics	chocolate and candy	cold medicine
toothpaste	bottled water	sunglasses
baby food	soda	toilet paper
cleaning products	greeting cards	magazines

CHAPTER 2

REVIEW AND EXPAND

ACTIVITY B PAGE 29

STUDENTS 2 AND 3: THE CUSTOMERS

Look at the list of items below. Each customer is shopping for the items on his or her list. Each customer should get the clerk's attention politely and ask for the first item on their list. Customers need to follow directions, locate the item in the store, and write the name of the item in the correct location on the map. Compare your completed map with Student 1 to see if you correctly located the item.

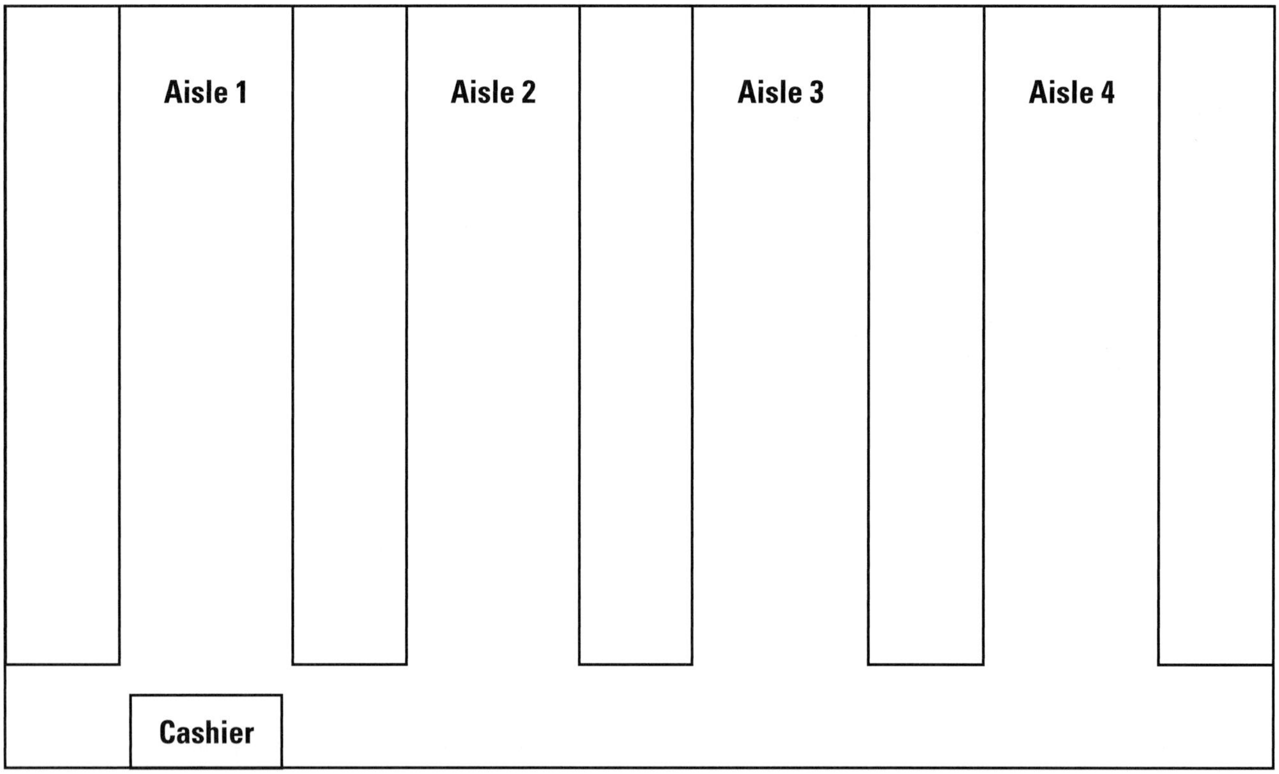

Aisle 1
Aisle 2
Aisle 3
Aisle 4
Cashier

Student 2's List	Student 3's List
cosmetics	soda
toothpaste	greeting cards
baby food	cold medicine
cleaning products	sunglasses
chocolate and candy	toilet paper
bottled water	magazines

CHAPTER 4

REVIEW AND EXPAND

ACTIVITY A PAGE 64

Work in groups of four. Student 1 should choose one of the problem cards below and explain the problem to the group.

Problem:

My neighbor is very noisy. He likes to listen to loud music. I need to study, but there is always too much noise.

Problem:

I don't know my grade on the test yet, even though I took the test two months ago.

Problem:

I want to take a few classes at the university, but my job is very demanding.

Problem:

I want to get a cat, but I live in an apartment complex that doesn't allow pets.

Problem:

My best friend calls me too much.

REVIEW AND EXPAND

ACTIVITY A PAGE 64

Students 2, 3 and 4 should use the cards below and write possible solutions to the problem. Students 2, 3 and 4 should each give a suggestion to solve the problem. Student 1 will respond to each suggestion and decide which suggestion best solves the problem.

Possible Solutions:

You	can		
You	could		
You	might want to		
You	may want to		
I	would		

Strong Necessity:

You	need to		
You	have to		
You	should		
You	have got to